Ladies of the Lake

Ladies of the Lake

Tales of transportation, tragedy, and triumph on Lake Chelan

Tom Hackenmiller

Point Publishing ....

LADIES OF THE LAKE: TALES OF TRANSPORTATION, TRAGEDY, AND TRIUMPH ON LAKE CHELAN

Copyright © 1998 by Tom Hackenmiller. All rights reserved. Printed in the United States. First edition.

ISBN 0-9663560-0-4

Library of Congress Catalog Card Number: 98-96026

For information:

>   Point Publishing
>   P. O. Box 355
>   Manson, WA 98831

Other books by Tom Hackenmiller:

>   *Wapato Heritage: The History of the Chelan and Entiat Indians* (Point Publishing, 1995)

Printed by Cascade Graphics
Wenatchee, Washington

Dedicated to the memory of George Pennell,
and all the men and women who have
contributed to the rich history of commercial
boating on Lake Chelan.

George Pennell (right), owner of the Lake Chelan Boat Company, 1942-1972, accepting a safety award on behalf of the company

Acknowledgments

I wish to thank the many people and organizations who provided me with information, material, photographs, and books that were so helpful in my research or the production and promotion of my book:

Alice Adams (Safeway), Alvin Anderson, Mark Beehler (North Central Washington Museum), Bill and Mary Bigelow, Ron Borchers (Cascade Graphics), Steve Byquist (KOZI Radio), Art Campbell, Jr. (Campbell's Resort), Central Washington University Library, Chelan Public Library, Nancy Clapp (Lake Chelan Boat Company), Christie Cook, Jim Courtney, Wes Crago, Cherie Crose (Wapato Point), Kathy Drinkwater (North Cascades National Bank), Cindy (Raines) Engstrom (Lake Chelan Boat Company), Evan and Myrt Griffith, C. J. Hackenmiller, Dan and Lynne Hunter, Tom Jacobson (Safeway), Chris Karapostoles, Lake Chelan Historical Society, Betty Lust (Lake Chelan Boat Company), Manson Public Library, Barb and Mark Marney, Keith Marney, North Central Washington Museum, North Central Washington Library, Jack Raines (Lake Chelan Boat Company), Shawn Raines (Lake Chelan Boat Company), Patty (Pennell) Risley, Lydia Rivers, Sandra Scribner (North Cascades National Bank), Ron Scutt (*Stehekin Choice*), Allen Shoemaker, Claude R. Southwick, Greg Stafford (North Cascades National Bank), Jarrod Stafford, Tacoma Public Library, Dick and Ginny Tessier, Chris Thorsen (Cascade Graphics), Rich Uhlhorn (*Chelan Valley Mirror*), University of Washington Library, Lou Verellen (Chelan Public Library), Washington State Surveyors General's Office, Washington State University Library, and Ken Wilsey (Lake Chelan Boat Company).

I especially want to thank my "editors," Jo Ellen Cook, Bill Jones, and Kathie Teeley who spent countless hours proofreading and offering valuable advice and suggestions.

Most importantly I would like to thank my wife, Kathie Teeley, for her encouragement and assistance throughout this project. The book could not have been done without her enthusiastic support.

Preface

When I moved to the Chelan Valley in the fall of 1986 my biggest concern was starting a new job as an English and Social Studies teacher at Chelan Middle School. It was a very hectic year which left me little time for pursuing interests outside school. The following summer on the Fourth of July my wife and I heard about an offer by the Lake Chelan Boat Company to ride the *Lady of the Lake II* to Manson Bay for the annual fireworks display. Thinking that a boat ride would be fun, we crowded aboard the *Lady* for an enjoyable evening. At the time, I never gave much thought about the boat or the history of transportation on Lake Chelan. As I taught over the years occasionally a student would venture to do a project about the old boats that plied the deep blue waters of the lake. I found the information very interesting and vowed to investigate the story of the boats someday.

Almost ten years passed before I would set foot on the *Lady of the Lake II* again. In the meantime, I had quit my job as a teacher and had written a book about the Chelan and Entiat Indians called *Wapato Heritage*. My only real contact with the boats was to watch the *Lady* and the new *Lady Express* as they glided by my home on Wapato Point or when they passed close by while I fished for lake trout on the "hump" offshore from Sunnybank. On the good days, when we got out on the lake early, we would hold up our catch to the toots of the big boat and the amazement of the wide-eyed tourists. Later we would listen to KOZI radio to hear the lake conditions summary by the boat's captain to see if our fish impressed him enough to get mentioned in his report.

In May of 1996, the Washington State Council of Social Studies Teachers asked me to give a talk about the local Native Americans to their members who had come to a conference in Chelan. The group had reserved the *Lady of the Lake II* for a couple of hours and wanted me to give my presentation while the boat cruised the lower lake. When I finished speaking I used the time to explore the large boat. I found a display near the front of the boat that briefly covered the history of some of the boats that had traveled the waters of Lake Chelan. Remembering my vow to research the boats, the subject for my next book was cemented.

Ladies of the Lake

The Lady of the Lake II at the Manson flag stop

In the summer of 1997 the Park Service in Stehekin scheduled me to give a talk about the Chelan Indians at their Golden West Lodge. Knowing that I was going to write a book about the boats, I decided to take the *Lady of the Lake II* to Stehekin. My wife and I anxiously waited with a small crowd at the flag stop in Manson to catch the boat. The boat was uncharacteristically late, but when she did appear her tardiness was apparent in her large number of passengers. We squeezed aboard and were soon on our way to Field's Point. When we arrived a huge crowd of people was waiting to board, including a young crew of approximately thirty men and women on their way to Lucerne to restore trails. Everyone seemed very interested in these young people and many spent much of the trip querying the trail crew about their work. Further up lake the boat stopped along the north shore to let off a man and his young son, both burdened with packs. The pair planned to venture into the wilderness for hiking and camping. The young boy was a favorite of the passengers and many shouted words of encouragement as he stumbled up the embankment towards the trail. Upon reaching the top, the small boy waved in triumph to the departing passengers and received a much deserved toot from the captain. After a couple of miles, the boat headed toward Canoe Creek on the north shore to release two more travelers who were going to visit friends at a cabin there. The crewmen bantered with those on shore as the boat neared and it was obvious that this was a frequent stop. From here, it was on to Lucerne where trucks and buses were waiting to take the trail crew to their camps. Tourists shouted good wishes to the departing trail workers who waved and broadly smiled in return.

Preface

Stehekin, 1997

The boat was soon on its way to Stehekin. Once there the throng of passengers disembarked from the boat as waiting vans and buses hurried the excited travelers off to tours of Rainbow Falls or to their mountain accommodations.

To me, what had at first been only a boat ride, quickly turned into the realization that the boats on Lake Chelan were not just transportation. They were the purveyors of a distinct culture formed from the isolation of the wilderness. As I began to investigate the impact of the boats it became immediately apparent that in early times these churning vessels were not just an attraction, but the lifeblood of the Chelan Valley. The boats and their owners were committed to commerce and to continuing the advancement of progress. The history of the boats and of the lake itself has always interested and fascinated people. The recent "Big Wave," controversy shows the strong attraction the boats and the lake have even today. This book is not just about the boats, but also explores the lure and lore of the lake itself and the activities that occurred around it. It is a story of fortitude through failure, and of, triumph over tragedy.

Table of Contents

Preface 9

Introduction 15

Section 1 - The Boats, 1889 - 1897 21

Section 2 - The Boats, 1900 - 1906 55

Section 3 - The Boats, 1910 - 1922 85

Section 4 - The Boats, 1929 - 1998 113

Section 5 - The Big Wave 153

Epilogue 163

Glossary of Boating Terms 165

Bibliography 167

Index 173

About the Author 175

Introduction

Chronicling the history of the boats that once navigated Lake Chelan has been a challenging task. Much is known about the later vessels, such as today's *Lady of the Lake II*, but there is often confusion about some of the earlier boats. There are many references to boats in early newspaper accounts, but at times, little or no information remains about some of them. The material included here mainly focuses on the better documented boats, but the lesser known crafts are mentioned as they relate to the others. Many sources were used to document the boats, including countless local newspaper articles and many personal interviews.

Details about the boats provided to the Lake Chelan Museum by Claude R. Southwick, and included in the museum's *History Notes* (Spring, 1988) article written by Hobbie Morehead, were especially helpful. Historical notes, by Robert Byrd in his book, *Lake Chelan in the 1890's,* were another very good source of information about the earliest boats. John Brown and Robert Ruby's book, *Ferryboats on the Columbia River*, provided excellent information about the early ferries that operated on the Columbia River. Finally, the *Chelan Valley Mirror* and the *Wenatchee World* newspapers have done an outstanding job documenting both the early and the later boats.

It should be noted that accounts about the boats by the *Chelan Falls Leader* and later the *Chelan Leader* newspapers often appear to embellish the facts. Boosterism was always a dimension in the early reporting, so at times these sources should be taken with a grain of salt. In most instances direct references are made to sources of information and the readers can judge for themselves their merit. As often happens with any historical account the material presented represents a likely scenario, but it may contain some inaccuracies. However, even if a fact or two is out of place or overly embellished, the reader will find that the following history faithfully elicits the spirit of commercial boating on Lake Chelan.

The book's first four sections are organized chronologically starting from the 1880s. In the early 1880s the region from Lake Chelan to the Canadian border had been designated as an Indian Reservation. By 1883 intrusion by whites into this area caused the federal government to rescind their agreement with the Indians. Three years later the government opened the former reservation lands to white settlement. The first section covers the years from 1889 to 1897, when white settlers and miners began coming to the Chelan Valley in greater

Ladies of the Lake

The first Lady of the Lake making a landing

numbers. Section Two covers the period from 1900 to 1906 which could be referred to as the "Golden Age" of commercial boating on Lake Chelan. It was during this time that the *Lady of the Lake*, the largest of the boats, operated on the lake. The next section chronicles the boats that were put into operation from 1910 to 1922. This era was a transitional period for commercial boating as the romantic old steamboats were phased out and replaced by gasoline powered boats. Section Four covers the years from 1929 to 1998 and it represents another transition from wooden boats to vessels made of steel and aluminum. Many of the boats launched during this period were either in operation or still owned by the Lake Chelan Boat Company in 1998. The final section of the book deals with the history of the various phenomena reportedly occurring on Lake Chelan over the years.

    Note: The year following the name of each boat in the headings refers to the year that particular boat was launched on Lake Chelan.

Chelan Valley Map

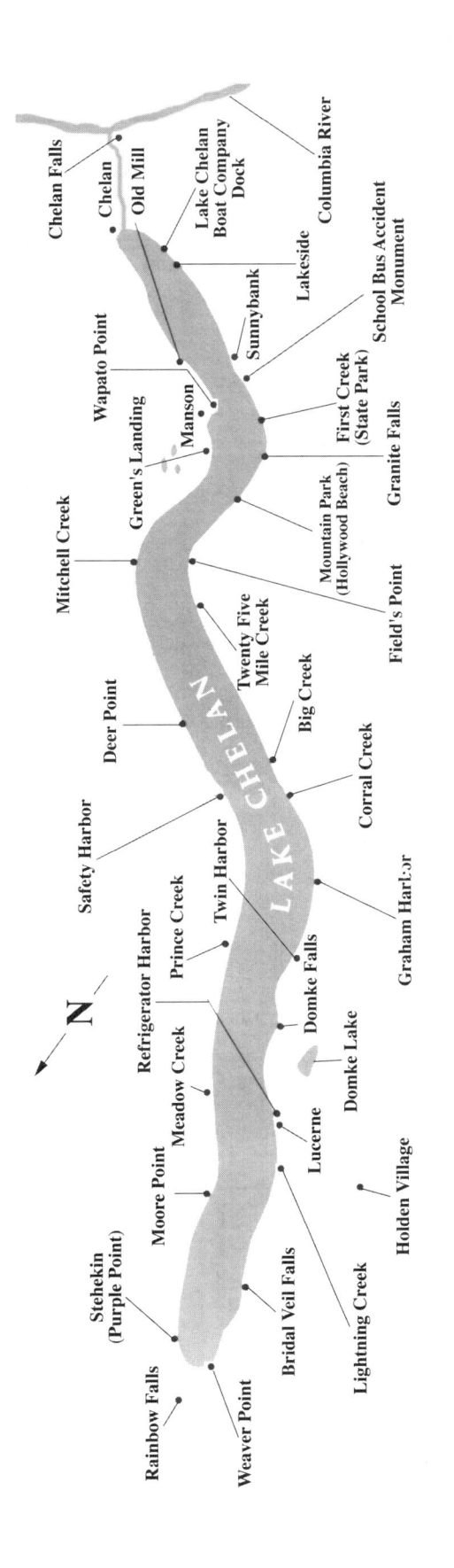

Ladies of the Lake

BOATS	SERVICE YEARS	L (FT)	W (FT)	DRAFT (FT)	ENGINE TYPE	SPEED (MPH)
Belle of Chelan	1889-1897	75	*	4	Steam	7
City of Omaha	1890-1912‡	34	8' 6"	*	Steam	10
Clipper	1891-1912	*	*	*	Steam	*
Queen of Chelan	1892-1893	55	10	*	Steam	*
Dragon/Dexter	1893-1904	60	12	3	Steam	8
Stehekin	1894-1904	72	16	4	Steam	11
Swan	1897-1913	72	15	4	Steam	10
Lady of the Lake	1900-1916	112	16	6	Steam	12
Flyer	1902-1906	60/85	14	4	Steam	12
Chechahko	1903-1906	55	10	2 1/2	Steam	11
Belle of Chelan	1905-1910	98	16	3	Steam	12
Tourist	1906-1916	64	11	4	Steam	12
Comet	1910-1929	42	8' 6"	*	Gasoline	*
May Bell/Princess	1911-1937‡	35/55	6	2 1/2	Gasoline	18
Spokane	1915-1921‡	70	10' 8"	*	Gasoline	16
Comanche	1915-1945	76	14	4	Gasoline	12
Mohawk	1916-1940‡	60	10' 6"	4	Gasoline	18
Liberty	1918-1957	45	9	*	Diesel	16
Victory	1919-1929	63	10	3 1/2	Gasoline	*
Cascade Flyer	1921-1944	63	9	3	Gasoline	30/16
Speedway	1929	62	12' 6"	3 1/2	Diesel	17
Lady of the Lake I	1945	65	17	4	Diesel	16
Lady of the Lake II	1976	100	24	6	Diesel	18
Lady Express	1990	65	21	5	Diesel	30
New Lady	1998	51	16	*	Diesel	50

*Unknown   ‡Approximate end of service

Introduction

Boat Timeline, 1889-1998

- (1889) Belle of Chelan
- City of Omaha
- Clipper
- Queen of Chelan
- Dexter/Dragon
- Stehekin
- Swan
- Lady of the Lake
- Flyer
- Chechahko
- Belle of Chelan
- Tourist
- Comet
- May Bell/Princess
- Spokane
- Comanche
- Mohawk
- Liberty
- Victory
- Cascade Flyer
- Speedway
- Lady of the Lake I
- Lady of the Lake II
- Lady Express
- New Lady

Section One
• • • • • • •

The Boats, 1889-1897

"For hour after hour the steamer glides along, awaking the echoes of her blasts, without a single evidence of the existence of man to be seen upon her lonely shores."
Lake Chelan visitor, 1891

Belle of Chelan, 1889

The *Belle*, as most of the early Chelan Valley residents called her, was the first of the commercial steamers to operate on Lake Chelan. Charles Follett and William Goggins, acting as an owner-operator team, built the wood burning steamboat during the fall and winter of 1888-1889 (Robert Byrd noted that before the *Belle*, H. W. Horton built and operated a sailing "yacht" that he launched from Stevenson's Landing at First Creek on September 24, 1888). Powering the steamer was machinery salvaged from a Columbia River ferry that had operated at the mouth of Colockum Creek. Launched in May of 1889 the *Belle of Chelan* was seventy-five feet long, and had a draft of four feet. Powered by an 1866 vintage ten horsepower Westinghouse oscillating steam engine, the *Belle* topped out at about seven miles per hour and sometimes used driftwood as fuel. The trip to the head of the lake and back took two days and required as many as twelve cords of wood for each trip. One of the first contracts for the new boat was to bring a boom of fir logs from Canada Point (now Purple Point) to L. H. Woodin's sawmill at Lake Park (present day Lakeside).

Christopher Robinson, who worked at Woodin's sawmill, remembered riding the *Belle* in 1890 and having the engine quit opposite of First Creek. The crew towed the boat to Williams' Harbor where they discovered that a valve-stem had broken. The sawmill was equipped with blacksmith tools so Robinson

Ladies of the Lake

Belle of Chelan at Moore's dock in 1892

and Charles Follett took a skiff back to the mill to make a new part. Once they finished the part the two men, accompanied by Charles Barron, rowed back to the steamboat. Arriving just after sunrise, the men quickly made the repairs. The *Belle* then steamed on its way to Stehekin, arriving just before dark.

In 1891 Follett and Goggins sold the *Belle* to the Lake Chelan Railroad and Navigation Company. That year the new owners outfitted the *Belle* with a new iron roof over her cabin. After the sale Goggins went to Seattle where he worked on the steamer *Greyhound*. A year later, Follett moved to Tacoma to act as chief engineer on the *Bailey Gatzert*. Follett later served as engineer on the Puget Sound steamer *Mountain Queen* on its Victoria run. Goggins would later return to work as chief engineer on the Columbia River steamer the *City of Ellensburgh*.

The newest owners of the *Belle* proved that the Chelan Valley was drawing interest from national investors. Edgar Allen, Andrew Hess, and Thomas D. Crane of Omaha, Nebraska; A. M. Cannon and E. J. Hale of Spokane; and L. H. Woodin and A. F. Nichols of Chelan organized the Lake Chelan Railroad and Navigation Company in 1891. Robert Law of Chicago acted as president of the company, Woodin served as vice president, and Edward Allen of Omaha served as secretary. The owners capitalized the new company by offering 15,000 shares at $100 each. If raised the $1,500,000 was to be used for construction

The Boats, 1889-1897

After Charles Follett sold the Belle he moved to Tacoma to serve as the chief engineer on the Bailey Gatzert (above)

and operation of a railroad in Okanogan County, the operation of steamboats on Lake Chelan and the Columbia River, the development of water power, and the sale of real estate. Besides the purchase of the *Belle*, the group planned to immediately build a narrow gauge railroad to the head of the lake to service the mines. The Lake Chelan Railroad and Navigation Company never built the railroad, nor did their many projects pan out, and the ambitious company was defunct within four years.

However, by the summer of 1891, the *Belle of Chelan* and another steamer named the *City of Omaha*, under superintendent A. F. Nichols of the Lake Chelan Railroad and Navigation Company, were making trips every other day to Stehekin. At this time the steamers normally landed on the south side of the Stehekin River. The following year the boats used the landing north of the river. The captain of the *Belle* was Charles J. Trow, with R. J. Watkins acting as chief engineer. Watkins was from Williamsport, Pennsylvania, where he worked as an "oil gauger." Trow once said that the *Belle* "hauled everything ... from tourists to prospectors and their saddle horses." An advertisement by the Lake

Ladies of the Lake

Chelan Railroad and Navigation Company in the *Chelan Falls Leader* in August of 1891 announced:

> **The Belle of Chelan ... makes regular trips to and from the head of the Lake, making close connections with all stages. The only direct and available route to the extensive Chelan mining district now coming into prominence. Horses and miners' supplies taken at reasonable rates.**

The ad went on in an attempt to cater to the tourists, "Special Inducements for Tourists. Special Excursion Trips Whenever Desired." By this time Woodin and Nichols had gone into partnership to operate both a general merchandise store and their Chelan Lumber Company at Lake Park. The store also acted as the headquarters for the Lake Chelan Railroad and Navigation Company.

The first excursion by the *Belle* occurred on Saturday, August 15, 1891, when seventy-three passengers journeyed to visit the Catholic church then located at what is today the Mill Bay Resort. Wapato John, patriarch of the Wapato family, had built the church in 1888. The purpose of the trip was for the townspeople to meet Father Etienne DeRougé, the Jesuit priest who ministered to the Native American churchgoers. A. F. Nichols had purposely set the fare to a very low amount of twenty-five cents to encourage participation. It was a festive day for both the Indians and the boat passengers. The excursionists spread out their lunch baskets, both on the shore and in the cabin of the steamer, sharing their contents along with an ample quantity of watermelons supplied by the gracious hosts. The young people danced and everyone enjoyed a wonderful day.

In 1891, tourism was already a focus to the growing towns of Chelan, Chelan Falls, Lake Park, and Stehekin. One visitor from the Coulee City area described the growing tourist trade this way, "this beautiful lake among the mountains ... [is] a place of resort for tourists, as well as a point of interest for miners and prospectors." Travelers coming from the East could take the U. S. Mail and Express stagecoach from Coulee City to Waterville and from there to Lake Chelan. Coulee City was the start of the stage route because it was the closest connecting point for the eastern portion of the Northern Pacific railroad system. The stage operator charged five dollars for the first leg of the journey and another two dollars to go from Waterville to Lake Chelan. On the final leg of the trip the stagecoach had to take a ferry, operated by two men named Dickson and Thompson (within a year A. W. LaChapelle and R. H. Lord operated the Chelan Falls ferry using a steam launch). The ferry went across the Columbia River to Chelan Falls and then the stage made the steep ascent to the lake. The

The Boats, 1889-1897

Alfred Downing's sketch of the Belle of Chelan, 1889

company's advertisement in the *Leader* touted Lake Chelan as being "noted for its fine scenery and good hunting and fishing, making it the best tourist point in the Northwest."

The hunting must have been good, because in the fall of 1891, the *Leader* reported that the steamer *Belle* had captured two deer trying to swim across Lake Chelan. "Deer hunting with a steamboat may be unusual but it is pretty good, all the same," the paper editorialized. Hunters routinely took the *Belle* for their hunting trips and it was not unusual to see mountain goats and bear lassoed to her deck.

Also that fall Clara Barton, founder of the American Red Cross, came to camp along the shores of Lake Chelan with three friends. Barton traveled by train from the East on the Great Northern Railroad to Spokane and then rode Northern Pacific's Central Washington branch to Coulee City. From there she remembered that they "crossed 'the Coulee,' a gorge which would be a canyon if it were not too wide — 75 miles long by three to five miles wide. We again took [the] stage and four horses and made the journey through to the Lake." Barton remarked that the road was difficult with "such dust as only the West can give, but the beautiful lake repays all the labor of reaching it." Another traveler described the stage ride as "a formidable trip ... [that] was a punishment for man and beast, and sheer crucifixion for a woman." From there Clara and her friends took the *Belle* for a three week stay at Moore Point, located six miles down lake from Stehekin on the lake's north shore. Barton, who was then in her seventies, was not unaccustomed to setting up tents and cooking afield.

She enjoyed her stay and later reminisced that "the lake and streams have plenty of fish, and the mountains plenty of game from the squirrel to the deer and bear, and you would think by the accoutrements, rods, lines, guns, revolvers, pouches and game bags that we might be anything from a troop of mountaineers to a band of brigands."

The stagecoach was just one of the ways to get to Lake Chelan; the other was taking the steamboat from Rock Island or Wenatchee. In the early 1890s the steamer *City of Ellensburgh* made two round-trips weekly up the Columbia River with stops at Chelan Falls. The vessel offered meals on board, and berths could be had for an additional fare. The steamboat made connections to both the stage to Ellensburgh, Washington (Ellensburg's name had an "h" at this time) and the Northern Pacific Railway line to Puget Sound. The cost to take the steamboat from Chelan Falls to Rock Island was $4.75, and if a passenger continued on by stage to Ellensburgh the total cost was $8.75. A trip on the steamboat from Rock Island to Chelan Falls would take nine hours traveling up river and only three hours heading back down. All the same, travelers were willing to make the long trip required to visit Lake Chelan.

By the summer of 1892, because of the increasing tourist demand and the burgeoning mining activity, the stage from Coulee City to Chelan Falls was increased to three times a week. Stehekin residents were especially happy with the increased traffic because the *Belle* had continued its regular schedule throughout the previous winter. A writer from Stehekin to the *Leader* in May of 1892 expressed this appreciation:

> **A year ago last winter steamboats were seldom seen at the head of the lake. Last winter the Belle made regular trips, some of which were no doubt made at a financial loss to her owners, but she came just the same, regardless of profit or loss, and we appreciate it. Capt. C. J. Trow has proved himself a friend indeed, and it is the desire of the citizens of this place to publicly express their gratitude for the manifest interest he took in our behalf during the past winter.**

The steamers on the lake were quickly becoming more than just transportation; they were a vital connection for the people in the Chelan Valley.

In the summer of 1892 the *Belle* played a prominent role in a unique funeral. The unusual services were held for D. W. Little, president of the Chelan Falls Water Power Company. At the time Mr. Little was in the process of building a home 200 feet above the lake at Granite Falls. He loved nature and was

The Boats, 1889-1897

Load of freight drawn by a ten-horse team from the steamboat at Chelan Falls on its way to Chelan

North Central Washington Museum, Wenatchee, WA

Ladies of the Lake

Columbia River steamboat map

especially fond of the wildflowers found around his lakeside residence. Mourners covered Little's casket with these flowers for his funeral. Many people attended the services held at Lake Park, and Judge J. M. Snow, A. F. Nichols, L. MacLean, Captain Charles Johnson, S. Edlund, Joseph Darnell, Howard A. Graham, and N. A. Meservey acted as pallbearers. Mr. Little's wishes were that his remains be interred at his favorite spot near his uncompleted home at Granite Falls. After the Lake Park services the pallbearers helped place Little's remains aboard the *Belle*. The deceased man's cherished steam yacht, the *Lady of the Lake*, then lead the funeral procession to Little's final resting place. Both vessels were draped in black and the *Belle's* flag flew at half-mast for the journey. The *Leader* headlined the event for its obituary written by J. Howard Watson as a "STRANGE FUNERAL CORTEGE," but it stands as a poignant example of how important the boats had become on Lake Chelan.

In the summer of 1892 the *Belle* was making daily trips to the head of the lake to keep pace with the growing tourist trade and the developing mining operations. Lake Chelan was becoming a very desired destination. As one early visitor remarked, "So confident are they in the future greatness of this lake that every little stretch of land is considered valuable." Superintendent Nichols even guaranteed that a special steamer would be used should anyone miss the scheduled runs because of poor connections. Lake Chelan had become a booming tourist attraction and the steamers operating on the lake were a large part of that success.

Despite the *Belle's* tremendous success, she did have her share of problems navigating Lake Chelan. In one 1892 incident the steamer lost her rudder while carrying a large load of passengers and towing a barge full of horses. The wind blew the boat into the rocks near First Creek. The steamers *City of Omaha* and the *Clipper* had to come to her assistance. The *Omaha* took on the passengers, as well as the barge, and continued up lake, while the *Clipper* towed the *Belle* back to Lake Park for repairs.

In August of 1893 under the headline, "Horseshoe Basin Invaded by a Party of Ladies and Gentlemen," the *Chelan Leader* reported on an excursion up lake by the *Belle*. The boat left Lakeside (Lake Park was renamed Lakeside that year) the morning of August 2, and took longer than usual to reach Stehekin because it towed a barge of horses. The forty-one passengers aboard the steamer included: Mr. and Mrs. C. C. Campbell, Rev. and Mrs. M. R. Brown (from Waterville), Mr. and Mrs. H. A. Graham, Mr. and Mrs. A. L. Johnson, Mr. and Mrs. Fred Pflaeging, Mr. and Mrs. C. Armstrong, Mrs. D. Little, Mrs. Ben F. Smith, Mrs. K. K. Ford, Mrs. C. E. Whaley; Misses Alma Lord, Edith Lord, Blanche Larrabee, Winnie Johnson, Lulu Hyatt, Myrtle Brown, Vevia Brown, and Jennie Higley; Messers. A. L. Woodin, C. D. Woodin, DeWitt C. Britt, W.

Ladies of the Lake

Burr Johnson, D. H. Lord, Stewart Johnson, Donald Ferguson, W. Z. Pepper, Sam Griswold, Ed Trow, Charles K. Ford, Arthur Campbell, Burt Johnson, and Professor J. T. Smith. The excursionists spent the night at M. E. Field's Argonaut Hotel which included an evening of music and dancing. The majority of the group used the horses brought up on the barge or those of Dan Devore's pack train for their trek into the Horseshoe Basin. After an adventuresome outing lasting three days the trekkers returned to the Argonaut for dinner and another evening of dancing. On Sunday morning the group happily boarded the *Belle* for their return home.

Also that year sixteen year old Nellie Little, who later married William Emerson, and a few of her friends took a rowboat to the head of the lake. She later recalled seeing the *Belle* traveling up lake on the opposite shore while they picnicked near a small creek. When the *Belle* put in for wood at Twin Harbor the girls hurriedly rowed across the lake to meet the steamer as it slowly moved away from the landing. The crewmen saw the girls and waited for them to come alongside and then gave them their mail. With that done, the steamer and the rowers continued on their way.

With the added interest in the Chelan Valley, the *Belle's* owners continued to operate her until they retired the boat in 1897. The *Belle's* proprietors removed her steam engine which was used to pump irrigation water. Later that year Herbert R. Kingman used some of the salvaged machinery from the *Belle* for his steamboat, the *Swan*. For many years the *Belle's* rotting hull could be seen in front of the Lake View House at Lakeside. It was a somewhat inglorious ending for the steamer that had piqued imaginations and gallantly served so many people in the Chelan Valley.

City of Omaha, 1890

The *City of Omaha* was the second steamer to run the waters of Lake Chelan. After a visit to Lake Chelan in 1889, Thomas R. Gibson of Fremont, Nebraska commissioned the building of this small steamer. Thomas D. Crane, a prominent Nebraska legislator, was the owner of the *Omaha* and later served as a member of the Lake Chelan Railroad and Navigation Company. That year Crane's Omaha company underwrote the $1,900 needed for the construction of the boat which was built in Waukegan, Illinois. When completed the oak hulled boat was thirty-four feet long and eight and one-half feet wide, and had a rated top speed of about ten miles per hour.

Gibson shipped the boat by railroad to Ellensburgh where the haulers moved the steamer by wagon over Colockum Pass to Wenatchee. From there

> **Lake Chelan Railroad and Navigation Company.**
>
> STEAMERS LEAVE EVERY OTHER DAY FOR ALL POINTS ON LAKE CHELAN.
>
> **City of Omaha and Belle of Chelan.**
>
> The Belle of Chelan, Captain C. J. Trow, makes regular trips to and from the head of the Lake, making close connections with all stages. The only direct and available route to the extensive Chelan mining district now coming into prominence. Horses and miners' supplies taken at reasonable rates.
>
> **Special Inducements for Tourists.**
>
> Special Excursion Trips Whenever Desired. Full Information Furnished on Application to
>
> **A. F. NICHOLS, General Supt.,**
> CHELAN, WASH.

Chelan Falls Leader advertisement, 1891

the shippers launched the *City of Omaha* on the Columbia River to make its journey to Chelan Falls. Here the steamer was hauled by wagon to Lake Chelan. Her maiden voyage occurred in the spring of 1890 when Howard A. Graham came out from Nebraska to assume control of the boat for his company. Eventually the *Omaha* operated as a mail boat under the control of the Lake Chelan Railroad and Navigation Company.

In the early 1890s Dan Devore, the well known Stehekin packer and miner, rode with his two horses on a barge pushed up lake by the *City of Omaha*. Devore had heard about the mining boom in the Horseshoe Basin and wanted in on the action. He said the trip took two days because of a prevailing down lake wind. Devore offered that the steamer "wasn't much of a boat," when asked about the *City of Omaha* thirty-five or forty years later.

In October of 1894 the *City of Omaha* rescued a survivor of a sailing accident on Lake Chelan. The incident occurred at dusk when two hunters, Ed Swearingen and L. S. Church, attempted to sail to Canoe Creek from Twin Harbor Creek on the lake's south shore. The boat made it to the middle of the lake, about a mile from land, when the wind suddenly lulled. Church went forward to take in the sail when a heavy swell rocked the craft sending him overboard and the boat rolling on its side. The wave also threw Swearingen into the cold water clear of the sailboat, but when he surfaced he could not see or hear his friend. Not being able to swim, Swearingen luckily had another wave propel him toward the stricken vessel. He spent most of the night clinging desperately to the overturned boat. Eventually Swearingen drifted ashore, but passed out as soon as he tried to walk. He awoke at daybreak with his feet still dangling in the water, but managed to start a fire to dry his clothes. Church was nowhere to be seen. At about ten o'clock, while on its morning mail run, the crew of the *Omaha* saw the stranded Swearingen and picked him up. The sail and Church's hat had drifted ashore, but rescuers did not find his body. "The body had not been recovered ... and probably never will be, as the lake at the scene of the accident is said to be over 1,000 feet deep, and these mountain lakes rarely or never give up their dead," the *Leader* matter-of-factly reported.

The *Omaha* operated commercially on Lake Chelan for many more years. Thomas R. Gibson gained control of the steamer after the Lake Chelan Railroad and Navigation Company ceased operations in 1895. Renamed the *Rustler*, Miss Elma Gibson often captained the boat with her father, Thomas, acting as the engineer. The Gibsons lived at Mountain Park which was fifteen miles up lake from Chelan on the south shore. Around this time Gibson may have leased the *Rustler* to two men named Devin and Steele who operated the steamer to haul wood.

In May of 1901 Gibson was involved in a amusing accident with the *Rustler*. While at his Mountain Park home Gibson decided to repair the boat in front of his house. There was a cottonwood tree that prevented him from positioning the *Rustler* where he wanted it for the repairs so Gibson tried to trim the tree from the boat. He tied a rope around the limb so that it would not fall on the *Rustler* when he sawed it off. Unfortunately this had the opposite effect and the large limb came crashing down on Gibson and the boat. Gibson received minor injuries in the episode, but suffered more from a bruised ego.

Around 1909 W. A. Hawley assumed control of the *Rustler* and used the boat to haul rafts of logs. On a Sunday afternoon in July Hawley and J. M. Bennett were towing a raft of telephone poles down lake for the Chelan Water Power Company. They encountered a fierce gale in the straits and had to seek safety in a sheltered harbor. When the *Rustler* and her crew did not arrive back in Lakeside as expected it was feared that she was lost. Adding to the concern was the fact that the *Lady of the Lake's* crew had not seen the boat on their down lake run. On Tuesday the *Rustler* and her crew were spotted making for Lakeside with only half of her raft of telephone phone poles as they had lost the other half in the storm.

The last mention of the *Rustler* was in June of 1912 when the *Leader* reported that she had sunk in front of the Tourist Hotel in Lakeside. Shortly after this Ralph Hawley raised the sunken craft, but it is not known what became of her. There is some speculation that her name may have been changed to the *Maid of Mountain Park* or the *Mayflower*.

Clipper, 1891

In 1891 Captain Charles Johnson and Thomas Gibson, associated with the Okanogan Realty and Investment Company, commissioned the launch *Clipper* for duty on Lake Chelan. The small steamer's former owners had previously used her to operate a ferry on the Columbia River. The *Clipper* worked the lake for a year or two and was used mostly to transport hunting and fishing parties or to tow barges of wood. Once in January of 1892, while the steamer was towing an overloaded barge of firewood, the barge sprung a leak and sank at Johnson's Point scattering wood adrift on the lake.

That spring the Burch Brothers of Wenatchee acquired control of the *Clipper*. Fred Barron captained the boat which also served in emergencies, once taking Fred Burch down to Chelan after he fell ill at First Creek. The *Clipper* was not always reliable as one report had her breaking down ten miles up lake from Chelan while taking a party consisting of Mr. and Mrs. George Cottrell, Mr. and Mrs. D. L. Gillespie, and Mrs. Snow fishing. A sailboat came to the assistance of the small launch and towed her back to the foot of the lake. In another incident, the *Clipper* had to return to Chelan after twice trying to plow through ice a foot thick just above Wapato Point.

In 1893 the Burchs' sold the *Clipper* to Frank Knapp to run his Columbia River ferry at the Navarre Coulee crossing. At the time it was almost impossible to follow the route along the river up to the Knapp's Hill Road, so the crossing was a popular southern route to Lake Chelan. The *Clipper* was the only ferry operating on the Columbia River during the flood of 1894. Knapp used five men to help him operate the ferry during the high water. While Knapp piloted the *Clipper*, one man fired her engine, and the other four men used poles to fend off debris raging down the river. The flood waters uprooted the home of Captain Griggs, owner of the Columbia and Okanogan Steamboat Company, at Virginia City (near present day Brewster), and was part of the mayhem that worked itself down river to Knapp's ferry landing.

Knapp sold the *Clipper* to Lewis Detwiler who used the launch in the Entiat area. The steamer changed hands a couple of times before Clyde Trapp purchased the *Clipper* in 1904 to operate his Orondo ferry. Trapp replaced the steam engine with a gasoline powered model, but after a time reverted to steam.

Ladies of the Lake

Frank Knapp's ferry, pushed by the Clipper, at the Navarre Coulee Crossing

In 1909 Trapp sold the *Clipper* to Earl Chandler who converted the power plant to a seven and one-half horsepower gasoline engine. The *Clipper's* interesting saga ended when she burned in 1912.

Queen of Chelan, 1892

In 1888 Charles, Fred and Louis Burch built the *Columbia Queen* at Birch Flat, just above the confluence of the Wenatchee River. The boat was fifty-five feet long and had a beam of ten feet. The following summer Charles and his son, Carl, traveled to Seattle to get the steam engine for the boat. After arranging to have the engine shipped they started on their return trip only to later learn that Seattle had burned to the ground on the day they left — June 6, 1889. Luckily, the fire did not prevent the delivery of the steam engine. The Burch brothers, along with their mother, Ellen, originally used the steamboat on their cross Columbia ferry run at Birch Flat. In July of 1891 the Burchs made an exploratory trip with the *Columbia Queen* up the Columbia River to the Okanogan River, but there is not any record of her subsequent use as a riverboat on that run.

Pioneer Square ruins of Seattle's fire on June 6, 1889

Ladies of the Lake

Columbia Queen on the Columbia River

When the Burchs retired the *Columbia Queen* from her ferry run they powered her up the Columbia River to Navarre Landing. Once there the brothers cut the boat in half, and using two wagons hauled it to the Smith Ranch near First Creek. Here the *Queen's* owners put her back together, and remodeled the craft into a vessel capable of carrying one hundred passengers. On October 20, 1892 the Burchs launched their boat, now renamed the *Queen of Chelan*, at Stevenson's Landing near First Creek. Charles Burch sold his share of the boat to Fred and Louis Burch who operated the company under the Burch Brothers name. Fred or Louis Burch would captain the *Queen*, with engineer Stuart Johnson and fireman Burt Johnson rounding out the crew. The steamer carried the mail, making two to three runs to Stehekin each week.

The Burch Brothers also operated the *Queen* as an excursion boat. The *Leader* reported that on the morning of June 25, 1893, the boat steamed out of Lakeside with a large group of excursionists. The weather was excellent as the *Queen* headed for Stehekin with ninety-four passengers and a crew of four. The following is a partial passenger list for the trip: Mr. and Mrs. Ben Smith and daughter, Mr. and Mrs. Pflaeging, Mr. and Mrs. George Cottrell, Mr. and Mrs. C. C. Campbell and son, Mr. and Mrs. Al Murdock and children, Mr. and Mrs. T. Hardenburgh, Mr. and Mrs. E. J. Porter, Mr. and Mrs. John Walsh, Mr. and Mrs. J. H. Hall, Mr. and Mrs. L. MacLean, Judge and Mrs. I. A. Navarre, Mr. and Mrs. J. T. Brownfield, Mr. and Mrs. Jim Gard, Mr. and Mrs. Stevenson, Mrs. Charles Johnson, Mrs. John Donaldson, Mrs. Higley, Mrs. A. S. Morrill, Mrs. Whaley; Misses Hyatt, Hardenburgh, Johnson, Mary Kelly, Winnie Johnson, Lulu Porter, Gracie Navarre, Sadie Powers, Astella Gard, Clara Ogle; Messers. Percy Wright, F. P. Eastburn, Ed Darnell, C. W. Young, Ira Ogle, Ed Ogle, Charles Powers, G. W. Brownfield, Arthur Gard, Tuttle, Banker, J. H. Watson, Emerson, Russell Pierpont, Joe Navarre, J. Macklson, W. J. Donaldson, Clarence Cottrell, R. S. Gorrill, Claude Johnson, W. Burr Johnson, W. T. Lovejoy,

The Boats, 1889-1897

The Queen of Chelan at the mouth of Fish Creek, 1892

J. B. Fosdick, J. H. Moos, J. W. Macy, E. J. Davis, A. L. Lindsay, Dell Larrabee, Volney Porter, Willard Pepper, Dick Irwin, O. D. Porter, and Gee Lee.

The *Queen's* excursion run arrived in Stehekin at 1:00 p.m. after making twelve stops. Not all the passengers traveled to the head of the lake preferring to stop at choice spots along the way to picnic and explore. Once at Stehekin many visited M. E. Field's hotel, the Argonaut, and six hearty individuals made the long walk to visit Rainbow Falls. At 7:00 p.m. the *Queen* started on her return trip, stopping along the way to pick up the picnickers, and made it to the foot of the lake at 11:15 p.m. The *Leader* ended its report of the trip by announcing that the Burch Brothers had another excursion planned for July 3.

Later that year in October a serious accident caused the *Queen* to sink near the lake's south shore across from Safety Harbor. By this time the Lake Chelan Navigation Company owned the steamer, but Fred Burch still captained the vessel. An account of the incident from *History of North Washington*, published in 1904, follows:

> **[The *Queen*] had gone to the head of the lake without unusual incidents, and was well down on her return trip. She had no passengers, and her crew consisted of Superintendent C. [J]. Trow, of the Navigation Company,**

Captain Fred R. Burch, and Engineer R. J. Watkins. Her freight was principally cordwood. Considerable wind was encountered, causing the boat to roll and pitch, and when about four miles from Safety Harbor, Superintendent Trow, who was at the wheel, felt the boat suddenly lurch to one side. As she did not immediately right herself he rushed down to the main deck to ascertain the cause. He found that the cargo of cordwood had shifted and that the water was pouring over the side into the hold. It was only a matter of a few minutes — perhaps seconds — until the steamer would fill and go to the bottom and there were no small boats or life preservers on board. Captain Burch had been hemmed in by falling wood and precious moments were consumed while brave men effected his release. Then Superintendent Trow, with rare presence of mind, managed to regain the pilot house and turned the steamer's head toward the south shore, which was barely gained when the boat sunk in sixteen feet of water. The crew did not have time to rescue even the mail sack, their food or bedding, and they were obliged to pass the night on the rocks without shelter. The upper works of the steamer went by the board at once, and floated away. Later the *Dragon* was signalled [sic] and the crew reached home.

R. J. Watkins may have rebuilt the *Queen* after her hull was raised, and rechristened the newly enlarged steamer the *Stehekin*.

Dragon / Dexter, 1893

In 1893 Joe Darnell, owner of the Lake View House Hotel, built the steamer *Dragon* for operation on Lake Chelan. The boat was a catamaran with a paddle wheel between her twin hulls. Darnell also acted as the boat's captain and Ed Darnell served as her engineer. The steamer was a multipurpose vessel, often making many unscheduled stops on her runs up lake. Some of the boat's many jobs included hauling wood for the Lakeside school, and bringing down loads of lime from Algie Higley's lime kiln for local building projects.

The *Leader* contained two interesting items involving the *Dragon* in 1895. One told the story of three men from Walla Walla who came to Lake Chelan in late November and stayed at the Lake View House. The itinerant

The Boats, 1889-1897

Steamer Dexter at Purple's Landing

adventurers were so impressed with the valley that they sold Darnell their horses and buggy and rode the *Dragon* up lake for a winter of hunting and fishing. The other item was actually an advertisement that Darnell placed in the *Leader* asking for a man or boy to "wheel smoke from the steamer Dragon." The ad proclaimed that Darnell was willing to pay the new hand six bits a day and all the food he could eat.

In addition to the *Dragon* there were several other boats in operation on Lake Chelan during this time. One was the steamer *Kitten* which was sunk by a large wave in September of 1899 (see Section Five: The Big Wave). Boat builder George Cottrell had a schooner named *Prosperity* that he used mainly as a pleasure craft. Also in use was a gasoline launch called the *Mountaineer* owned by Ellery Fosdick. She was most likely used to perform transport services on the lake between Lakeside and Chelan. Launches were used when traveling to Chelan because the lake was very shallow below Lakeside. In the spring the water was so low that sand bars were above the water. There was a narrow channel near the south shore deep enough for the smaller boats to navigate through to Foote's Landing which was out from where the Forest Service buildings are today.

Ladies of the Lake

Splash-board dam with the original Woodin Ave Bridge in the background

In 1898 M. M. Kingman and other Chelan businessmen financed the building of a splash-board dam that raised the lake level three feet. M. E. Field, owner of the Field Hotel (formerly the Argonaut) in Stehekin, was a prominent member of the state legislature and was successful in limiting the height of the dam to prevent flooding of his up lake holdings. The raised lake level allowed for the larger steamboats to navigate to Chelan resulting in a significant increase in business there. To accommodate this new boat traffic the town had erected a dock just below the future site of Campbell's Hotel Chelan. When the hotel was completed in 1901 the dock was immensely beneficial and convenient for the hotel and its guests. However, the drive to build the dam and dock caused a lot of animosity between the towns of Chelan and Lakeside. Many Lakeside residents refused to use the dock because they believed their town should be the center of activity in the Chelan Valley.

In the summer before the dam's construction Darnell sold the *Dragon* to A. J. Dexter who rebuilt the boat and renamed it the *Dexter*. Her new owner relaunched the renovated boat in March of 1898. The remodeled steamer still had the catamaran hull, pushed by an inset chain-driven sternwheeler, and powered by a thirty horsepower twin Oscillator engine. The *Dexter* was sixty feet long, twelve feet wide, and had a draft of three feet. Usually employing a crew of two, the boat could reach a speed of eight miles per hour. The crew chiefly used the *Dexter* to tow rafts of logs from up lake to the Kingman-Sullins sawmill at Lakeside. A. J. Dexter acted as the captain of his sternwheeler and Ed Merritt was the chief engineer. Ben Little and Captain Olsen also piloted the boat for Dexter. Other crewmen on the boat included engineers, Samuel Thornton and Ray O'Neal.

In February of 1899 Dexter fitted the *Dexter* with a large pile driver. By the next July Dexter reported that he was doing a booming business for the year having already put in over 150 piles for wharves. His passenger count also rose that year as he lowered his round-trip Stehekin fare from $2.00 to $1.50. His luck turned in October when the *Dexter* sank in shallow water at Granite Falls after the craft had taken on a load of furniture for Mrs. C. E. Little. George Cottrell went up to assist Dexter in raising the waterlogged boat. Not wishing to lose any more business than he had to, Dexter had the craft recaulked and back in the water by the middle of December.

The *Dexter* hosted a Sunday stag fishing party to First Creek in May of 1901. The group included Judge C. C. Campbell, A. H. Murdock, and D. D. Bowman, of Chelan; and Judge William Henry, N. Z. Palmer, and Captain Dexter, of Lakeside. Although the fishermen had good supply of the "right kind" of bait they did not do very well.

The Dexter at Prince Creek, Domke Mountain in the background

Ladies of the Lake

In December the *Dexter* was involved in an amusing incident involving a cow owned by a man named Doc Fleming. Captain Olsen was at the helm of the boat when the cow broke loose and climbed through a freight room window. None of the crew saw this transpire, but surmised this is what happened when all they found of the cow was its broken rope. The *Leader* tongue-in-cheek reported, "Captain Olsen threw out the life buoys, but whether the calfie sank to the depths of the ultra marine blue or swam ashore — thereby hangs the calf's tale." The cow never reappeared and the *Dexter* got on with business later that month hauling down a load of Christmas trees.

Cutting ice on Lake Chelan

During early February of 1902 Dexter used his boat to fulfill a contract to put up 100 tons of ice for Lyman R. Colt. Colt, one of the heirs of the Colt gun manufacturing company, had built a large cold storage plant near his home located above Rose Beach. That fall Steve Ryan, once an engineer on the Lake Chelan steamer *Flyer*, was rumored to have purchased a half-interest in the *Dexter*. The business transaction was never confirmed nor denied.

The following year Dexter spent quite a bit of money overhauling his boat. He had H. M. Christie do work on the *Dexter's* engine and later C. T. Ryan spent time making general repairs to the boat. Unfortunately it was all for naught as the *Dexter* sank in the middle of July in 1904. The vessel sprung a leak in shallow water on the lake's south shore nineteen miles up lake near what was then referred to as the old Christie place. At the time Dexter said he doubted if he would raise the boat because it was old and rotting. As an afterthought, he said he might consider raising the boat in the winter when the water level dropped.

Dexter never recovered the aging and exhausted old steamer. He tried to continue his business by leasing the steamer *Swan*, then owned by W. D. Richards of the Richards Lumber Company. However, by February of 1905 Dexter returned the boat to Richards, probably because the added lease payments made it hard to make a profit. Captain Dexter's colorful story of steamboating on Lake Chelan ended later that month when he and his wife moved to Dayton, Washington to "resume" the business of brick making.

Stehekin, 1894

R. J. Watkins, in partnership with Captain Stewart Johnson, built the *Stehekin* in 1894. Watkins, a native of Pennsylvania, was an experienced steamboater having operated them for years on the Great Lakes before coming to Chelan in 1889. Johnson would later move to northern British Columbia where he captained the Hudson Bay Company steamer, *Mount Royal*, on the Skeena River. In the early 1900s Captain Johnson was in command of the *Mount Royal* when it struck a rock in the river. The swirling currents broke the luxurious craft in two and six people lost their lives in the only major disaster befalling a steamer on the dangerous Skeena River. Luckily for the *Stehekin* no such calamity occurred while Johnson operated it on Lake Chelan.

The sternwheeling *Stehekin* was seventy-two feet long, sixteen feet wide, and drew about four feet of water. She had a double flue and a twin shotgun engine with a five foot stroke that was powered by a Scotch Marine Boiler. The boat had a top speed of approximately eleven miles per hour. To power the vessel the crew usually made firewood stops at First Creek, Twenty Five Mile Creek, Lucerne, Moore Point, and Stehekin. Many early settlers made extra money by providing wood for the steamer.

Watkins, who also acted as the *Stehekin's* captain, built the boat with a double deck. The top deck was for passengers and the lower deck was used to haul freight, stock, rowboats, and other supplies needed for the prospectors and residents living up lake. Dan Devore, the Stehekin packer, used the boat to transport his close to thirty horses to be wintered down lake. The *Stehekin*, which had the mail contract, made three trips a week to the head of the lake manned by a crew of four. Passengers wishing to ride round-trip to Stehekin paid four dollars.

Ladies of the Lake

Sternwheeler Stehekin taking on cordwood

Roy Barton, who later captained the *Tourist* and the *Lady of the Lake*, worked as a fireman on the *Stehekin*. When Barton quit Watkins replaced him with a man named Fleming. Other crew members at various times included first mate, Otis Darnell; chief engineer, Ed Merritt; fireman, Ray Smith; and pursers, Fred Pflaeging, Bernard Devlin, and Fred Ripley. Mr. and Mrs. J. J. Zook and their replacements, Mr. and Mrs. Budd, also worked on the boat — possibly as cooks. Mrs. Barbara Schearer, owner of the Mountain Home hotel at Bridge Creek, was in charge of the galley and dining room. Watkins also hired a Japanese cook from Seattle who worked for a short time on the *Stehekin* until he "yumped his yob," as the *Leader* tactlessly reported.

In 1894 Lake Chelan remained a prime vacation destination and travelers would go to great lengths to get to the lake. E. I. Denny traveled to Chelan that fall from Seattle and penned that a trip across the continent might have been easier. "A part of the route was dangerous, a part uncomfortable, rough, and wearisome," Denny wrote in his travelogue which appeared in *The Northwest* magazine two years later. Denny's route had taken him over the famous railroad switch-backs on Stevens Pass and on to Wenatchee. From there he boarded the *City of Ellensburgh* for a very eventful trip to Chelan Falls. Trouble began when the Mississippi style steamboat with two large smokestacks reached the Entiat Rapids. Here the Columbia River split into three channels and making

City of Ellensburgh, struggling up the Columbia River

headway was often very difficult. Denny's own explanation of the events is worth noting:

> At the E-ti-at rapids we enriched our experience. There the main stream is invaded by the En-ti-at-qua [Entiat] River, a bar and small island dividing the Columbia into three channels. With I do not know what pressure of stream, an attempt was made to run the rapids. The furnace roared, the engine rattled and the boat paddled in midstream, almost evenly matched with the current, only to drop back into a eddy where she stuck on a shoal. Captain and crew went out on the bar, put a hawser around a big drift-log, and started the engine. But this only seemed to make matters worse. They then rigged a pry astern and pushed off, to start up stream and repeat the failure. At the third or fourth trial the boat drifted back, and then came a shock as of giant hands bending the vessel's frame ... It was growing dark, and our situation was not reassuring. The prospect of being blown up, or else swept away in the boiling rapids was not agreeable to contemplate. Finally there were hurrying feet and shouts, and all at once we shot off again

into the hissing current. After a while it was decided to tie up behind the island, upon which decision we retired to rest.

At dawn the next day, by means of a kedge and cable put out on the island, the rapids were overcome safely and easily and about twenty four hours were spent between Wenatchee and Chelan Falls.

Once at Chelan Falls Denny's adventure continued. After a "perilous and unpleasant ride" to Lakeside, possibly provided by the Farley Transfer Company, Denny retired for the evening at the Lake View House. Having had a refreshing night's sleep the traveler boarded the *Stehekin* at eight o'clock for his trip to Railroad Creek. Denny noted that, "navigation of the lake seems pleasant and safe, although the icy depths do not look inviting, and a pile of cork jackets in the cabin of the 'Stehekin' were suggestive as well as reassuring." He continued, "No wharves appear and none are needed, as the steamers land anywhere, owing to the depth of the near shore." Denny spent three weeks camping on the lake, staying for the first snow of the season on the lower Railroad Creek. His trip back to the coast was less eventful, and included an afternoon of searching for arrowheads along the Chelan River while waiting for the steamboat to Wenatchee.

The residents of the Chelan Valley often used the steamboats in times of emergency. One Sunday morning in late January of 1895 V. H. Behne accidentally shot J. Frank Cochran as the men prepared to go hunting. The incident took place on Cochran's ranch which was on the north side of the lake about twenty-five miles from Chelan. Over Cochran's objections his partner carried him into his nearby cabin. When Behne asked the fifty-seven year old victim if he thought he would recover, he replied: "No, I shall never get over it." Fearing the worst Behne rushed down to the lake and rowed across to William Hurn's ranch. Here he found Louis Meier and sent him by rowboat to fetch a doctor and the steamer. Behne then returned to Cochran's with William Hurn, but the wounded man was dead when they arrived. Dan Devore and George Taylor had also found Cochran's body and were at the cabin. In the meantime Meier's rowboat had filled with water compelling him to walk much of the way to Lakeside. Once there, Meier found Dr. Hayley and told him about the accident. Soon the doctor and H. N. Merritt were aboard the *Stehekin* and the boat got underway by 9:00 p.m. reaching the Cochran place at about 11:00 p.m. Finding Cochran dead the rescuers loaded his body aboard the *Stehekin* and headed back to Chelan, arriving there at 2:00 a.m. Monday morning. The justice of the peace, E. B. Peaslee, as acting Okanogan County coroner, ordered a coroner's

The Boats, 1889-1897

***Steamer Stehekin at Missouri Harbor (across from Green's Landing)
on the south shore of Lake Chelan***

inquest to be held at the scene of the accident that day. The jury (consisting of C. C. Campbell, H. A. Graham, William Hurn, H. N. Merritt, Joseph A. Graham, and Louis Meier) and the witnesses took the steamer *Omaha* to Cochran's. The jury determined that the bullet had accidentally discharged from Behne's gun, hit a knot in the wall and then split into two fragments. One fragment lodged in a nearby saddle, while the other hit and killed Cochran. After ruling on the shooting the jury and witnesses reboarded the *Omaha* and returned to Chelan arriving at 2:00 a.m. Tuesday morning. Early frontier emergencies could at times be very time consuming, while frontier justice, on the other hand, often transpired expeditiously.

Later that year the *Stehekin* hosted a delegation of the Washington State Road Commission. J. Howard Watson of First Creek served on this committee which at the time was studying the feasibility of constructing a wagon road across the North Cascades. The committee traveled to Fairhaven (Bellingham) in July and spent four weeks checking out various routes for the road. Much of their time was spent in the Thunder Creek and Slate Pass regions which is in the area where the present North Cascades Highway now runs. On August 12 the group arrived at the head of the lake and boarded the *Stehekin* for its down lake run. At the time the commissioners considered using Lake Chelan as the outlet for the state wagon road to cut construction costs. J. Howard Watson's recommendation was for the road to be built over Rainy Pass. The full commission eventually chose a route over Cascade Pass, and authorized the building of a twelve and one-half mile road from Stehekin to Bridge Creek. Work began on the Cascade Pass route in 1896, but it never amounted to more than a four foot horse trail. Almost eight decades later the North Cascades Highway would finally open using the route Watson had originally suggested.

St. Andrew's Episcopal Church

In 1896 community volunteers started logging the timber for St. Andrew's Episcopal Church and they used the *Stehekin* to transport the logs. Christopher Robinson headed up the crew that harvested the logs on the slide above Mountain Park. Ben Smith and William Boyd used the steamer to take their horse team up to the logging camp to join with William Hurn's team to haul logs down to the shore. Once the *Stehekin* deposited the logs at Lakeside, A. H. Murdock and his friends peeled the bark from the logs. In 1897, under the able leadership of Rev. W. H. Roots, volunteers rented the Kingman-Sullins sawmill for a day and were able to process the lumber in record time. The church was designed by the famous New York architect, Stanford White (a

The Boats, 1889-1897

friend of Roots, who designed New York's original Madison Square Garden), and held its first service on Christmas Eve of 1898.

In October of 1897 Captain Stewart Johnson sold Watkins his share of the *Stehekin*. The following February Watkins used the vessel to tow down a raft of exceptionally fine logs which he planned to saw into planking along with other lumber to be used to remodel the craft. He hired an expert craftsman, Dave Steele, to do most of the work. The *Stehekin's* pilothouse was moved atop the roof of the top deck. Steele then added a smoking room just ahead of the ladies cabin and a galley aft. The galley had a stove and Watkins planned to serve meals to the passengers. Watkins elegantly furnished the women's cabin with moveable deck chairs, a sofa, and even a grand piano for entertainment. In July of 1898 Watkins beached his steamboat to replace her aging hull and do additional overhauling. After the remodeling, the *Stehekin* could easily accommodate seventy-five passengers. Watkins relaunched the renovated vessel at the end of August.

The *Chelan Leader* on March 10, 1899 reported this curious event involving the *Stehekin*:

> **Captain Charles J. Trow, of the steamer Stehekin, reports an incident on the trip up last Monday that borders on the phenomenal. It is well known that Lake Chelan rarely freezes over even in the coldest weather, and for the past 10 or 15 nights it has hardly frosted. On Monday morning the thermometer registered about 45 above zero. Yet the steamer people found a thin skim of ice, perhaps a quarter of a mile wide, frozen clear across the lake between Johnson's point and Rose Beach and also another from above Sunnybank across to Wapato Point. It was remarked on the boat at the time that should they come back and tell of it they wouldn't be believed. It is accounted for only on the supposition that the night must have been absolutely still and that cold currents from the coulees combined with the glacial waters to form ice on the glassy surface of the lake.**

The article went on to say that this type of activity had never been heard of before and that it might not occur again in 100 years.

It was a busy and varied year in 1901 for the *Stehekin* and her crew. On March 26 the craft hosted an excursion to the head of the lake. For a three dollar fare passengers got a round-trip ride on the boat, a grand ball and dinner

Ladies of the Lake

Stehekin steaming across Lake Chelan

at the Field Hotel, and a night's lodging. In the middle of May the steamer hauled down fourteen tons of Higley & Isenhart Brothers' lime to Lakeside. In June the *Stehekin* took a Sunday excursion to Mountain Park for a picnic — the fare was a reasonable twenty-five cents and children were free. Later in the month the boat took a load of lumber up lake for the Field Hotel.

It was also a year for unusual incidents. In May of 1901 a curious thing happened one night on the *Stehekin*. The boat was docked at the wharf and Captain Watkins allowed a young man, Billy McGregor, to sleep on the deck. The next morning Watkins discovered that the man's bed roll had not been slept in and that McGregor was nowhere to be found. Watkins, thinking that maybe the man had fallen overboard, searched the water all around the boat to no avail. It is not known if McGregor was ever seen or heard from again.

Later that summer the *Stehekin's* crew narrowly averted a tragic accident at the Stehekin dock. The steamer was slowly approaching the pier when two boys in a canoe ran afoul of the boat's paddle wheel. The wheel quickly overturned the canoe throwing one of the boys into some bushes that he used to pull himself ashore. The other boy desperately grabbed onto the paddle wheel and clung on for dear life as the wheel slowly circulated. Hearing the boy's screams, the crew quickly shut down the revolving paddle wheel and rescued the boy. Other than a good dunking, the young lad was perfectly all right.

The Boats, 1889-1897

In July of 1901 Watkins sold a half-interest in the *Stehekin* to Ben F. Smith. Later Smith would acquire total ownership of the steamer when Watkins went to work as an engineer for the Columbia & Okanogan Steamship Company. During the last week of 1902 the *Stehekin* filled with water and sank at the Lakeside dock. Smith and a crew of men successfully raised the vessel the next week. Smith then rented the *Stehekin* to the Logan family to use as their residence.

In May of 1903 Smith sold the *Stehekin* to E. E. Shotwell who used the craft as a barge. Her owner retired the *Stehekin* in 1904 because of old age and the next year she was burned to the water line, then filled with rocks and sunk. Shotwell sold the machinery from the *Stehekin* to buyers in Sand Point, Idaho who planned to use it on a steamer there. The *Stehekin's* aging hull can still be seen on the north side of the old Howe Sound Dock when the lake level is down.

Swan, 1897

In the fall of 1897 Herbert R. Kingman, owner of the Kingman-Sullin sawmill in Lakeside, started construction of the *Swan* using parts and machinery salvaged from the old *Belle of Chelan*. Kingman had initially hired a master shipwright from Seattle, but shortly after starting the job the man unexpectedly returned to Puget Sound. Earl Larrabee was also working on the *Swan*, but he did not have enough experience to complete the boat. Kingman then contracted with the Cottrell Boatyard in Lakeside to finish the *Swan*. Their boatyard was located about where the three fingers of fill now extend into the lake between Chelan and Lakeside. Captain Stewart Johnson helped with the caulking for the new boat and John Carlyle painted the hull.

Before the boat builders even completed the *Swan,* H. R. Kingman sold a one-half interest in the mail steamboat to Morrison M. Kingman and leased him his remaining share for four years. On March 14, 1898 Kingman launched the *Swan* for her inaugural cruise. The screw driven *Swan* was seventy-two feet long, fifteen feet wide, and had a draft of four feet. Her wide beam gave her a slightly "tubby" appearance. A one cylinder upright engine with a Scotch Marine Boiler powered the *Swan.* With a cruising speed of ten miles per hour, her three man crew generally used her to deliver mail and to tow logs to the Kingman-Sullin sawmill. H. R. Kingman and a Mr. Laurance operated the vessel.

The *Swan* soon assumed her role as the sawmill's log boom tow boat. In April of 1898 a large raft of logs under tow by the *Swan* broke up in heavy winds off of Deer Point. It was too windy to round up the logs that day so the

Ladies of the Lake

The Swan docked, and the Stehekin underway from Moore Point

crew headed the boat back to Lakeside. The next day they returned with the *Swan* and recovered 205 out of the 212 logs they had lost the day before and successfully towed them to the sawmill.

During this time the Kingman-Sullin sawmill also retailed their lumber. Payment for lumber included just about anything. Old records showed that the company traded lumber for eggs, cabbage, and potatoes. The mill sold thirty-two foot lengths of two inch thick lumber for only sixty-four cents. Of course, wages then amounted to about $1.50 to $2.00 per day.

On one winter trip between Lakeside and Granite Falls the *Swan* plowed into heavy ice that pierced her hull. The enterprising crew used sacks of flower to plug the hole. Unfortunately these provisions were part of a load that Mrs. Roy Barton and Miss Little were then taking home.

In late November of 1899 the *Swan's* owners beached her to "have a new wheel put on." While she was out of the water workers thoroughly overhauled her upper works to prepare her for the following season. The *Swan* was soon at work towing rafts of logs down lake. These rafts could be as large as 600,000 feet of lumber, but averaged about 125,000. It would take the *Swan*

The Boats, 1889-1897

Swan, Stehekin, and Darnell's Lake View House Hotel in Lakeside

about thirty-one hours of running time to bring an average sized raft down from the head of the lake.

When not towing logs H. R. Kingman often carried summer excursionists up lake on the *Swan*. On one of these trips in August of 1901 the *Swan* took a group of travelers to Moore Point. Shortly after Kingman had docked the steamer one of the passengers, Mrs. Ridenour, accidentally dropped her baby over the railing. The baby plunged into the water between the dock and the boat. Hearing the commotion Kingman quickly jumped to the dock and was able to pluck the infant out of the water when it bobbed to the surface. The baby had "no more serious consequences than a ducking," but Mrs. Ridenour was a nervous wreck until Kingman returned the child safely to her.

In June of 1902 W. D. Richards, owner of the Richards Lumber Company, purchased the *Swan* from Kingman. The first thing Richards did was to have a contractor, named Dodge, remodel the *Swan* by adding a cabin on her second deck. This work was done to make the boat ready to replace the *Flyer* on the Stehekin run. The *Flyer*, built the previous year, had been found unsuitable for the rough water sometimes encountered in the straits.

During the spring of 1904 Captain Richard W. Riddle replanked, painted, and generally repaired the *Swan*. That summer season Richards leased the steamer to the Pershall Brothers who planned to use the boat for up lake excursions. One round-trip to Stehekin in June of 1904 had excursionists dancing to the sounds of the Chelan Cornet Band at the Field Hotel for a $2.00 fare. The Pershalls operated the *Swan* until the middle of August when they discontinued its run because it was not profitable. The next year Captain A. J. Dexter leased the boat for a short time, but discontinued in February because the boat was still not making a profit.

Raft of logs in what is today called Mill Bay

After Dexter returned the *Swan,* Richards continued to use her to tow logs to his Lakeside sawmill. That summer the *Swan* brought down the largest raft ever recorded on the lake — 600,000 feet of logs. The lumber was the property of M. E. Field and W. F. Purple who planned to use the wood for their building projects. Field used his lumber to expand his landmark hotel. In 1906 the *Leader* reported that the *Swan* was "waterlogged and unfit for service," but a short article in June of the following year reported that the boat towed down a "big raft" of logs.

Richards eventually sold the *Swan* to Dan Vroman, who in 1913 resold the boat to Don Mathers for fifty dollars. Mathers used the boiler from the boat at his brickyard which he operated just above what is now the Chelan Concrete Company. He then beached and burned the *Swan.*

Section Two

•••••••

The Boats, 1900-1906

*"It may be dusty, but an outing is
no outing without dust."*
***Chelan visitor describing the stage ride
to Chelan Falls in 1904***

Lady of the Lake, 1900

Charles H. and H. H. Allger, two brothers from Tacoma, began construction on the first *Lady of the Lake* in May of 1900. Before the boat's completion the Allgers sold a third of an interest in the vessel to M. S. Berry. Her owners may have named the vessel after D. W. Little's launch which he operated on the lake in the early 1890s. It was a popular name, as there was another *Lady of the Lake* operating on the West Seattle to Seattle passenger ferry run at the time. That boat burned on the water in the early 1900s, and afterward was rebuilt as the steam tug, *Ruth*.

Christopher Robinson "Robin" Switzer remembered seeing the *Lady of the Lake* under construction near the "frog pond" in Lakeside. He said that the day of the launching, August 25, 1900, was a festive one with several hundred people attending and a dance planned for later in the day. Eleven year old Gretchen Purple, daughter of Mr. and Mrs. W. F. Purple (Mr. Purple had been one of the workmen on the boat), broke a bottle of wine over the bow as she said, "I christen thee Lady of the Lake." At this point the new boat was supposed to glide into the water, but after the workers released the chocks the boat stuck to the soft shore. The *Stehekin* was used to try and pull the *Lady* out, but the line broke before she could be set free. With the help of all available manpower and with a pull from the *Swan* the *Lady* finally took to the water the next day. To get the boat loose the crew had generously applied axle grease and used jackscrews to help ease the boat into the lake.

Lake Chelan's flagship was 112 feet long, sixteen feet wide, with a six foot draft. She was — and is — the largest boat to ever operate on the lake. The boat builders used windows, doors, and other equipment from the Puget Sound ferry *Vashon* in the *Lady's* construction. The Allgers shipped in lumber from Puget Sound to be used in the new boat. Captain Richard W. Riddle oversaw the construction of the steamer for the Allger brothers. The boat had a three cylinder 250 horsepower fore and aft compound steam engine that turned a five foot diameter, four blade, iron propeller. At full speed the propeller turned 300 revolutions per minute. Her Roberts type pipe boilers were capable of furnishing 125 to 150 pounds of steam to two engines of this capacity. The engine required eight to ten cords of wood, costing about fifteen dollars, to make the round-trip to Stehekin. The *Lady* had a cruising speed of approximately twelve miles per hour.

At the time, people considered the new steamer the ultimate in appearance and efficiency. This is how the *Leader* described the new boat after her launching:

> **There will be a cabin and freight room forward of the boilers and engine, which set amidships, and a ladies cabin aft. She [has] only one deck at present but will add another as soon as business justifies it. She is painted white with red hull and green water line, and sits on the water like a duck. The cost when completed, will be nearly $8,000. She will make the round trip to Stehekin and back in one day. There is about one more week's work on her and then she will make her trial trip.**
>
> **Just under the front window of the pilot house is a pine limb on which can be seen a bird's nest. A pair of King birds built their nest on a limb overshadowing the bow of the boat, commencing about the same time the keel was laid, and in spite of all the noise built their nest and raised their flock of little ones. As they were seen so constantly day after day they seemed to become part of the boat, so when she was ready to launch the limb was sawed off and nest and all were carefully fastened to the pilot house.**

The finishing work took longer than expected. After the builders put in and adjusted the smoke stack on the *Lady* the *Leader* commented, "It is predicted

The Boats, 1900-1906

The Lady of the Lake with a single deck, an upper cabin was added in 1903

that she will be easily the swiftest boat on either the lake or the Columbia River." On Saturday, September 15, 1900, Ben Little piloted the *Lady of the Lake* on her trial trip to Wapato Point and back. Five days later the new steamer took its first load of excursionists to the head of the lake.

By the middle of May of 1901 the *Lady of the Lake* was making three round-trips per week to Stehekin. The steamer went up lake, leaving from Lakeside at 8 a.m., on Tuesdays, Thursdays, and Saturdays. The boat left Stehekin at 7 a.m. on Wednesdays and Fridays, and at 2 p.m. on Saturdays. This schedule, when meshed with that of the steamer *Stehekin,* provided for daily boat service to the head of the lake. Besides the regularly scheduled trips the *Lady* provided excursions. One *Leader* advertisement for a picnic trip to Twenty Five Mile Creek by the Allgers listed a fare of fifty cents and enticed the public by proclaiming, "That's cheaper than staying at home." In a June newspaper promotion the Allgers advertised a Friday night moonlight excursion for twenty-five cents. The entertainment for that particular trip had Miss Blanche Emerson performing the Highland Fling for the passengers.

In October of 1902 Captain E. E. Shotwell, manager and part owner of the Lake Chelan Navigation Company, purchased the *Lady of the Lake* from the Allgers. M. S. Berry maintained his share of the *Lady* and Ben F. Smith also became a partner in the new boat company. In the spring of the following year the company had the steamer remodeled by adding an upper deck with an elegant ladies cabin, a smoking room, and a captain's compartment. The total cost of the improvements came to over $3,500, with a total investment between $10,000 and $15,000. Captain Richard Riddle was in charge of the remodeling and his son, Hiram A. Riddle, came from Seattle to help his father with the job. Riddle's son acted as foreman of the twelve to fifteen men who worked on the project. Some of the workmen on the remodel included R. J. Riley, Andrew Crumrine, G. A. Benson, Harvey Thompson, C. W. Van Meter, Robert Osborne, Roy Barton, and painter, John Carlyle.

Shotwell claimed the *Lady of the Lake* could now easily accommodate 200 passengers with a crew of four or five men. A round-trip to Stehekin usually took two days because of all the required mail, freight, and passenger stops. During the *Lady's* tenure on the lake the freight included apples from growers in the Twenty Five Mile Creek area and the Buckner Orchard in Stehekin. The growers in these areas did their own packing and the boxes loaded on the boat were ready for market.

Mrs. Barbara Shearer, known as "Mama Shearer," served as a cook aboard the *Lady of the Lake*. A native of Switzerland, Shearer later operated a hotel and boarding house owned by the Chelan Transportation and Smelting Company where Railroad Creek entered into Lake Chelan. She called the hotel the Lucerne House because the beautiful scenery reminded her of Switzerland. The need for lodging at the Lucerne landing had intensified after 1901 when the Chelan Transportation and Smelting Company began a survey for the narrow gauge railroad to haul ore from the Holden claims. The company abandoned the railroad project when it later went bankrupt. Shearer would eventually become Lucerne's first postmistress, operating the post office in the lobby of the hotel. Workers dismantled the hotel in 1921-22 with the lumber later used to build a pavilion over the lake. Heavy snows in the early 1950s eventually destroyed the pavilion.

Around 1901 C. T. Conover brought his family from Seattle to Lake Chelan for a summer vacation which included a ride on the *Lady of the Lake*. After reaching Wenatchee by train the family checked into the Bell Hotel. The family spent the night being devoured by blood thirsty mosquitos and arose at four o'clock in the morning to catch the steamer *Selkirk*. Once in the dining room for breakfast Conover noticed that fly paper adorned the walls and pillars to which masses of flies had met their sticky deaths. He remarked that such a sight was not appetizing especially after his mosquito induced sleepless night.

The *Selkirk* steamed up the Columbia River until it got stuck in the Entiat Rapids. After taking a cable ashore the crew was able to get the riverboat

The Boats, 1900-1906

The Lady of the Lake being loaded with fruit from the Rosedale Ranch, near Twenty Five Mile Creek, in 1907

North Central Washington Museum, Wenatchee, WA

Ladies of the Lake

Columbia River steamer, Selkirk, struggling up the Entiat Rapids

through the rapids using the boat's powered capstan (like a winch). Once at Chelan Falls the steamer deposited the family right on the sandy shore as there were no docks. In the midday sun a four-horse stage took the group up the perilous hills to Lakeside — all the while enveloping them in a cloud of alkali dust. The experience was too much for Mrs. Conover whose husband had to revive her with aromatic spirits of ammonia upon their arrival. Riding with the Conovers was another family with several children, which was a theatrical group scheduled to perform "East Lynn" at the schoolhouse that evening.

After spending the evening at their Lakeside hotel the family boarded the *Lady of the Lake* at seven o'clock the next morning for their trip to the head of the lake. Conover described the voyage: "The farther one progressed the more the scenery unfolded, and we were soon on a shimmering emerald sea lined with rugged mountains, many snow-capped. Chelan is unquestionably one of the loveliest lakes in the world." Arriving at Stehekin at one o'clock in the afternoon the family quickly settled into the Field Hotel for an enjoyable stay. Conover remarked that the family's return trip down the Columbia River, which had taken them nine hours to ascend, took only three hours to Wenatchee. He said that a race between their steamboat and another with brooms tied to her mastheads enlivened the trip.

The Boats, 1900-1906

Steamship Columbia at the Chelan Falls Landing, 1905

Ladies of the Lake

Four-horse stage rounding the "Cape Horn Turn" on its way from Chelan Falls to Chelan

Another visitor to Lake Chelan penned his travel experiences in the December 1904 issue of *Wilhelm's Magazine*. The writer had traveled to Wenatchee by train and described the steamboat ride as "delightful." At Chelan Falls a four-horse stage met J. A. Gard's wharf boat that had taken the passengers from the steamer to the sandy shore. After an hour's ride "over a wild and picturesque roadway built around rocky, precipitous points and over deep gorges and along stony canyons," they reached the town of Chelan. Here the stage pulled up in front of C. C. Campbell's Hotel Chelan in what the writer described as "an event of daily interest."

After a night's stay and a hasty breakfast at the hotel, the traveler boarded H. C. Keeler's launch, *The Imp*, at the Chelan dock for a smooth run to the Lake Chelan Navigation Company's headquarters at Lakeside. Here he boarded the *Lady of the Lake* for its run to Stehekin. The writer described the *Lady* as a "representative steamer and is fitted throughout for elegance, comfort and ... for equipment is not equaled by many ocean going craft." The steamer made many mail stops and it surprised the traveler how the boat could "shove its nose up to the shore at almost any spot, whether upon the rocks or a pebbly beach, and load and unload." The boat arrived in Stehekin at about 3:30 in the afternoon

The Boats, 1900-1906

and the writer checked into the Field Hotel. Later in the day Ben Smith, the steamer's purser, displayed the fish he caught on the Stehekin River after the crew had secured the boat. Other crew members at this time included Lou Ward, Kid Almandinger, and Ray O'Neal, Sr.

Hotel Chelan and the old Woodin Ave Bridge

After an enjoyable stay up lake the traveler returned to Lakeside. He described the stage ride as the "feature" of the trip from Lakeside to Chelan. "After crossing the Chelan River the driver directs his four horses up a steep embankment to the Hotel Chelan, when at the crack of the whip they clamber up and draw after them the heavy stage ... a touch of excitement lasting for a moment," he wrote. The next morning after a night's stay at the hotel, Arthur Gard's stage took the writer and other passengers to Chelan Falls. "It may be dusty, but an outing is no outing without dust," the traveler penned. Soon the steamboat gathered the passengers and freight and headed down the river. The travel exposé ended with these words of encouragement for other would be adventurers: "When the hot and sultry days of summer come, here can be found a cool and quiet nook. Who would seek the grand, the wonderful and the beautiful should not pass by but visit Lake Chelan." Many would continue to take this advice for years to come.

Ladies of the Lake

Lady of the Lake loading members of the Epworth League at Lakeside for their annual excursion (the man in the white shirt at the end of the gangplank is Robert Little, and the man standing on the right in the white shirt is captain, Roy Barton)

Roy Barton began captaining the *Lady of the Lake* in 1906. When he came to the Chelan Valley six years earlier he had worked as an assayer at Railroad Creek. His first experience as a steamboat crew member was as a fireman on the *Stehekin*. Other crew members over the years included Ben Little, pilot; Chauncey W. Van Meter, engineer; Charles Wolverton, alternate engineer; Lyle Van Meter, Ray O'Neal and A. A. Ten Eycke, firemen; Fred Ripley, purser; and Bert Huey, deckhand. In Barton's first year as captain of the *Lady* he saved her from a fire that ravaged two other steamers, the *Chechahko* and the *Flyer,* burning them both to their waterlines. Barton saw the flames from his Lakeside home and rushed to jump on the *Lady* which was moored next to the burning boats. After he and others cut the *Lady* free they got her out into the lake away from the danger.

In the spring of 1906 E. E. Shotwell replaced the *Lady of the Lake's* engine with a more fuel efficient model. Shotwell bought the new engine from the Puget Sound Dry Dock & Machine Company of Tacoma. The new power plant was a 200 horsepower 9x22x14 fore and aft compound condensing engine with twin Roberts Boilers. This reduced her fuel needs almost in half; a round-trip to Stehekin now only required four or five cords of wood.

The Boats, 1900-1906

Tram built on the mountainside near Coyote Creek to bring logs down to Lake Chelan where they were formed into rafts to be towed down lake

In the following years the *Lady of the Lake* became a workhorse on Lake Chelan. Her runs included taking educators up lake for their annual Teacher's Institute, to hauling 4,500 sheep from the Hunter & Allyn herd to Grade Creek on the lake's north shore. Other jobs included hauling Dan Devore's pack horses from Stehekin to Lucerne, transporting a carload of R. P. Wright's apples to Lakeside, and towing a 100,000 foot raft of logs from Coyote Creek to the Pennell & Garton Sawmill in Lakeside. A more sedate duty had the *Lady* transporting the remains of a six year old Seattle boy down lake. The boy had died in a horse riding accident while on a trail ride near Bridge Creek. The *Lady of the Lake* was a constant presence on Lake Chelan. In some ways she defined the Chelan Valley's ever increasing populace — determined, dependable and hard working. Elsewhere the railroads had ended much of the need for riverboats, but on Lake Chelan the romantic era of steamboating continued awhile longer.

Ladies of the Lake

The completion of the railroad from Wenatchee to Oroville in 1914 essentially ended the steamboat era on the Columbia River. Louis Hill, son of Great Northern's founder, Jim Hill, once told C. C. Campbell that the line was not economical for the railroad company, but it was part of his famous father's dream. Yet the railroad's arrival at Chelan Falls Station only increased the number of visitors willing to come to Chelan and ride the steamboats there. The Great Northern Railroad would buy the Field Hotel two years later, and actively promoted tourism to Lake Chelan. A Great Northern tourist brochure touted the new accessibility to Lake Chelan:

The completion from Wenatchee, Washington on the transcontinental line of the Great Northern Railway, northward alongside the Columbia River of the Great Northern's Wenatchee-Oroville line, and the inauguration on the new line of conveniently-scheduled trains, has made accessible to the tourist another wonder place of America: Lake Chelan in the Cascade Mountains. In the past reached only after a laborious trip by steamboat against the swift current of the Columbia and a tedious climb by horse-stage, and after a number of inconvenient lay-overs enroute, Lake Chelan from all points in the Pacific Northwest over Great Northern rails is now quickly and comfortably reached, and for the transcontinental passengers via the Great Northern is now from Wenatchee a short and easy side-trip.... The Oroville line train, after a run of little over an hour alongside the Columbia, reaches Chelan Station at 6:15 p.m., from which point auto-busses, leaving immediately after arrival of the train, transfer passengers to Chelan and Lakeside at the foot of the lake.

The brochure listed the Lake Chelan Navigation Company's summer schedule for the *Lady of the Lake* and the gasoline powered boat the *Comanche*. The boats left daily, except Sundays, at 7:30 a.m. arriving in Stehekin at 3:00 p.m. Down lake trips left at 7:00 a.m. arriving in Lakeside at 3:00 p.m. Besides these schedules the motorboat *May Bell*, piloted by Captain Burley, provided an express service. Capable of a top speed of eighteen miles per hour, the express boat ran on the same days as their other boats, but left Lakeside at 1:00 p.m. and arrived in Stehekin at 4:30 p.m. For the down lake run the express boat left at 6:00 a.m. and arrived in Lakeside at 10:00 a.m. The *May Bell's* schedule

The Boats, 1900-1906

The Field Hotel

Ladies of the Lake

Lady of the Lake docked at Lakeside

allowed travelers to make their Great Northern train connection without the necessity of an overnight stay at either Lakeside or Chelan. Besides the boat schedules the Great Northern brochure promoted horseback riding, hunting, and camping trips in the Cascades. These side trips, costing from $5.00 per person per day and up, were anything from a four day trek to the North Fork of Bridge Creek to an eight day adventure to Glacier Peak.

In 1915 Roy Barton and Chauncey W. Van Meter went into partnership with E. E. Shotwell in his Lake Chelan Transportation Company. Barton captained the *Lady of the Lake's* last runs during the bitterly cold winter of 1915-16. On one trip up lake on January 31 an eight inch thick sheet of ice blocked the *Lady's* return to Lakeside until February 27, 1916. During this time mail for those up lake from Manson had to be taken by bobsled to Green's Landing, located a few miles above the town. For two weeks after her return, the barge used to cut the channel was sent ahead of the steamer to break the trail. This was done to prevent the ice from ripping a hole through the hull of the steamer.

Later in 1916 the transportation company retired the aging *Lady of the Lake*. Workers dismantled the once elegant steamer with the engine sent to Seattle and her wheelhouse added to Roy Barton's Lakeside home. Salvagers burned the stripped *Lady* to the water line at the west end of what is now Lakeside Park, and then sunk her with a load of rocks. The hull was still visible as late as the 1950s. The *Lady of the Lake's* passing marked the end of the steamboat era on Lake Chelan. It would be thirty years before another *Lady of the Lake* navigated the waters of Lake Chelan.

Flyer, 1902

In the fall of 1901 Captain Richard W. Riddle, who came to the Chelan Valley from Puget Sound the year before to build the *Lady of the Lake*, started construction of the *Flyer*. Prior to coming to the valley Riddle had built many steamers on Lake Washington, including the tug *Mascot* and the steamers, *Abe Perkins* and *Enigma*. He captained the latter for eight years on Lake Washington and Puget Sound. Riddle not only built the *Flyer*, but he later served as the engineer in charge of the Lake Chelan Navigation Company's boat fleet.

Captain R. J. Watkins and Ben F. Smith commissioned Riddle to build the *Flyer*. Construction began in November of 1901 after Watkins used the *Stehekin* to bring down a huge fir crook to be used as the stem of the new boat.

Flyer paddling past Missouri Harbor

Ladies of the Lake

Flyer docked at Granite Falls

By the middle of December Riddle was supervising a crew of eight men working on the vessel. When completed the *Flyer* was the second sternwheeler to run on Lake Chelan. Her owners, who had the mail contract on the lake, launched the boat at the end of June in 1902.

The new craft was sixty feet long, had a beam of fourteen feet, and drew about four feet of water. The *Leader* reported that her machinery was identical to that of the Columbia River steamer *Camano*, except that the *Flyer's* boiler was fifty percent larger. It is interesting to note that a month before the *Flyer's* launching the *Camano* went down in the Entiat Rapids. The sinking occurred after a load of wheat and wood shifted allowing the strong current to overturn the vessel. One of the *Camano's* crewmen drowned in that incident.

Soon after Watkins and Smith put the *Flyer* on the Stehekin run they discovered that her design was unsuitable for the often rigorous conditions found up lake. Riddle had designed the *Flyer* to navigate the shallow water between Lakeside and Chelan, but the dual need to run shallow and in rough water were incompatible. The owners decided to contract with George Cottrell to rebuild the sternwheeler. Cottrell's contract called for cutting the boat in half and adding an additional twenty-five feet which would give the boat a final length of eighty-five feet. At the end of July, while the *Flyer* was at Cottrell's, his boatyard burned to the ground after a fire started in Bernard Devlin's machine shop next door. The *Stehekin* arrived on the scene and the crew used her steam engine to pump water on the blaze. The launch *Imp* was also used to bring fire extinguishers from Chelan to fight the fire. Although the *Flyer* suffered only minor scorching, it did portend trouble ahead for the craft.

The Boats, 1900-1906

The steamers Lady of the Lake, Stehekin, and Flyer at the Lakeside dock, 1902

Ladies of the Lake

A plucky Cottrell was quickly back in business repairing the *Flyer*. An advertisement for Cottrell's Boat House in the *Leader* shortly after the fire read: "Yes, we got burned out and badly scorched, but our boats are all right." The announcement underscored the prevalent determined attitude found in the Chelan Valley at the time.

Cottrell refloated the *Flyer* in September of 1902 and soon her owners had her back on the Stehekin run. The craft, operated by a crew of four, had a top speed of about twelve miles per hour. Captain Watkins served as the boat's captain, Steve Ryan acted as the engineer, and Ben F. Smith was the purser. Russell Pierpont also served in some capacity on the boat.

In the spring of 1905 E. E. Shotwell's Lake Chelan Navigation Company took control of the *Flyer*. Ben F. Smith, who had been a partner in the company, quit to pursue other interests. With the change of ownership Captain Shotwell piloted the boat, Chauncey Van Meter served as engineer, and Fred Ripley performed as purser.

With the heavy influx of miners in the early 1900s the *Flyer* made three trips weekly to the head of the lake. The sternwheeler carried mining supplies, mail, and many travelers enroute to the hotels up lake. A spectacular fire on April 2, 1906, at one o'clock in the morning destroyed the *Flyer* as she sat docked together with the *Chechahko* and the *Lady of the Lake*. The inferno originated on the *Chechahko* when a fire started under the boiler. Charles Wolverton, Ray O'Neal, and Ben Little were asleep on the *Flyer* when the flames awakened them. Along with Roy Barton, who had come from his house, the group saved the *Lady*, but the fire ruined both the *Chechahko* and the *Flyer*.

Chechahko, 1903

Captain Richard W. Riddle built the steamer *Chechahko* (there are several variations found in the spelling of this boat's name) in 1903 for the Lake Chelan Navigation Company. Riddle employed a crew of fifteen men to build the steamer. The crew included J. L. Davis, Pete Robichaud, and H. H. Hunt, with Joe Henritzi painting the new craft. The workers completed the boat at the end of May and her trial trip proved to be successful. Her owners claimed that the *Chechahko* was the first boat to make a maiden trip to Stehekin without experiencing any glitches.

The *Chechahko* was fifty-five feet log, ten feet wide, and produced a draft of two and a half feet. The vessel could travel approximately eleven miles per hour powered by her fore and aft steam engine. She had a very bright and distinctive white paint job which made her glisten in the sunlight. People of the era said the steamer could be seen for miles — especially in the straits.

The Boats, 1900-1906

Chechahko cruising along

Richard (Dieterich) C. Hulseman remembered returning to Lake Chelan from Minnesota to live on a ranch near Twenty Five Mile Creek. His father, Dieterich H. Hulseman, had purchased the land from William Gibson in 1900. The Hulseman family first moved to the ranch shortly after acquiring the property. However, the family returned to Minnesota after Richard's mother, Louisa, gave birth to a daughter a year after their arrival. The Hulsemans moved back to the Midwest because Richard's mother was uncomfortable living in an area that was twenty miles by boat to the nearest doctor.

On their return to Lake Chelan in 1903, the Hulsemans and their four children, ranging in age from about one to ten years old, rode on the Great Northern Railroad to Wenatchee. There the family took rooms for the night at the Bell Hotel. At four o'clock the next morning the family boarded the riverboat, *North Star*, for the trip to Chelan. The river was running high and fast and the riverboat's crew had to cable the boat through the Entiat Rapids. When the family arrived at Cobb's Landing, just below Chelan Falls, they boarded Art Mather's four-horse stage for the trip to Lakeside. After spending the night at Joseph Darnell's Lake View Hotel they took the *Chechahko* the remaining twenty miles to their ranch.

The Lake Chelan Navigation Company used the *Chechahko* mostly as an auxiliary and charter boat. One highlight was when the company used the new steamer to take Congressman F. W. Cushman and his wife to Stehekin in July of 1903. Later the *Chechahko* hosted a delegation of Great Northern Railroad officials to the head of the lake. For the most part the vessel performed more mundane tasks like hauling apples, lime, lumber, and other freight.

Ladies of the Lake

Flyer, Chechahko, and Lady of the Lake

The Boats, 1900-1906

The boat company also used the *Chechahko* to transport passengers between Chelan and Lakeside because her smaller draft allowed the boat to easily navigate the shallow channel between the towns. The small steamer also served to accommodate the increasing influx of miners flocking to the Chelan Valley at this time. As mentioned earlier, the *Chechahko* burned along with the *Flyer* on August 2, 1906, when a fire erupted under her boiler.

Belle of Chelan, 1905

In 1904 the first mayor of Chelan, Amos Edmunds, and Captain August H. Bergman, from Bergman, Minnesota, formed the Lake Chelan Steamboat and Transportation Company. The new company had set ambitious goals for capital projects in the region, including producing electrical power and the operation of electric railways, but their first aim was to build a new Lake Chelan steamboat. Bergman had operated steamboats on Lake Bergman in his home state and was no stranger to the building and operation of steamers. By the end of the year Bergman had ordered the new boat's steam engines from the St. Paul Machine Works in St. Paul, Minnesota. The new engines would possess the latest technology and would be twin, 6x12x8s of a compound condensing type. The engines' builder, George P. Kahlert, calculated that the engines would develop 208 horsepower at 300 revolutions per minute.

Belle of Chelan

Ladies of the Lake

Amos Edmunds ordered Puget Sound lumber for the new steamboat in February of 1905. In April Captain Bergman and his family moved to Chelan from Minnesota. Later that month the machinery and lumber arrived at Chelan Falls. The supplies were then hauled to Chelan where the construction of the boat would take place at a wharf west of the M. M. Foote residence. Edmunds projected that the new steamboat would be ninety-eight feet long, have a sixteen foot beam, and a draft of three feet.

To raise money for their new venture Edmunds and Bergman held a meeting in the middle of April at the Hotel Chelan to attract investors. They explained to those in attendance that they intended to incorporate with a capital stock worth $20,000 at one dollar per share. The capitalists then offered 12,000 shares of stock for immediate sale. Edmunds had earlier estimated that the new boat would cost $12,000 to build. Bergman bought 3,300 shares and Edmunds another 1,000 — making them the majority stockholders. Other stockholders included C. C. Campbell, Homer Dunning, Norman Higgins, John Isenhart, G. L. Richardson, H. W. Van Slyke, and C. E. Whaley.

The Lake Chelan Steamboat and Transportation Company had contracted with George Cottrell to build their new steamer. Cottrell and his crew were soon progressing at a rapid rate and by the middle of May they were ready to launch the hull. By mid-June the crew was already installing the boat's upper cabin. Trial trips at the end of June proved to be successful and the boat was almost done. Even before the boat was christened it performed an emergency mission by taking Charley Wapato to Green's Landing which was near his Falls View home. Wapato had severely injured himself in a riding accident and his doctor did not expect him to live (Wapato did recover completely, only to be murdered a year later).

With the boat nearing completion Edmunds asked the local chapter of the Women's Christian Temperance Union (W.C.T.U.) to host the christening ceremony. The W.C.T.U., with Mrs. Ellen Farley in charge of the event, held the christening at the Chelan dock on the morning of July 12, 1905. After an introductory speech by Mayor Edmunds, Miss Florence Bergman sang, "The Building of the Ship." Following the song Miss Julia Bergman broke a bottle of Rainbow Falls water on the boat's anchor and christened the new steamer the *Belle of Chelan*. After the ceremony members of the W.C.T.U. and the boat company's stockholders took an excursion to First Creek on the *Belle*.

The newest *Belle of Chelan* was double decked with a pilothouse on top. The *Belle's* steam engines powered her twin screws giving her a cruising speed of approximately twelve miles per hour. A five and one-half ton Scotch Marine Boiler that was five feet in diameter and fourteen feet long provided the steam for the engines. The *Belle's* main cabin included a library and writing

The Boats, 1900-1906

Belle of Chelan at the Chelan dock with the Campbell's Hotel Chelan in the background

desk, and the floors showcased carpets made in Brussels. Her crew consisted of pilot August Bergman and his two sons: Oscar, acting as the engineer and Walter, serving as the purser. C. T. Black managed the operation of the boat.

Besides the *Belle's* duties of taking supplies and passengers up lake, her owners used her for moonlight excursions during the summer months. The first excursion for the *Belle of Chelan* took place two days after her christening. It was a moonlight cruise to First Creek which left Chelan at 7:30 p.m. and returned at 10:00 p.m. The fare for adults was twenty-five cents and only fifteen cents for children. By November August Bergman reported that the *Belle* was making expenses, plus a "trifle" more.

The *Belle of Chelan* had a hard time operating on the lake because her limited draft made the boat difficult to control in the wind. The boat had been purposely designed this way to navigate the shallow waters below Lakeside to Chelan. George M. Parrish once recalled that on a summer day in the *Belle's* first year of operation he watched Bergman try to make a landing with the boat at Prince Creek. There was a hard wind blowing when Bergman let off power as the boat neared the landing. Suddenly a gust of wind overtook the *Belle* throwing her sideways upon the beach. The abrupt landing did not damage the steamer and her crew quickly had the boat underway. Soon after this incident

Ladies of the Lake

Belle of Chelan and Lady of the Lake at the Lakeside steamboat headquarters

The Boats, 1900-1906

Belle of Chelan and Tourist docked below Campbell's Hotel Chelan

the *Belle of Chelan* did not show up on her regular run. When the crew of the *Lady of the Lake* learned of the *Belle's* problems they tied a broom to the *Lady's* mast. This was a common steamboating practice which signified that a rival boat had one-upped or made a "clean sweep" of the competition.

In June of 1906 the Lake Chelan Steamboat and Transportation Company negotiated with E. E. Shotwell to allow the *Belle of Chelan* to use his company's dock facilities at Lakeside. That May the *Belle* resumed her regular summer schedule after George C. Walker overhauled the boat. On one up lake trip the steamer took a large cargo of new furniture for the newly remodeled Field Hotel. In November stockholders elected a new board of trustees for their struggling transportation company. The new trustees were August Bergman, B. Stillwell, Emil Weber, Theodore Lind, and Oscar Bergman. By this time Amos Edmunds had disassociated himself from the group and had formed another boat company.

In April of 1907 Bergman spent considerable time and money repairing the *Belle of Chelan*. By May the *Leader* reported that Bergman was taking the steamer to Stehekin three days a week — Mondays, Wednesdays, and Fridays. Two months later Bergman threw in the towel declaring that he could not make a profit unless he could base his boat company in Chelan. He said this was not possible because the Chelan town council did not maintain the Chelan River at a sufficient depth for year round operation of a large steamboat. E. E. Shotwell

Ladies of the Lake

bought Bergman's stock in the boat and took control of the craft.

In 1910 Shotwell had the *Belle of Chelan* towed from Lakeside to Chelan after having salvaged her machinery. The boat was tied up at a piling near a bathhouse, just up the channel from the Pennell sawmill, located between Chelan and Lakeside. In 1912 the *Belle* hosted her last excursion for the Methodist Episcopal Church. The church members decorated the boat with Japanese lanterns for the evening "cruise." Of course the *Belle* never went anywhere that night as she sat moored in six inches of water with her keel buried in the sand. The *Leader* reported that the church group had a great time all the same on the *Belle's* last adventure. The *Belle* sat deteriorating for many years until the clearing of the shoreline in anticipation of the completion of the dam in 1927. Workers burned the old *Belle* and the rising waters covered her remains.

Tourist, 1906

In 1906 a group of Chelan businessmen headed by Amos Edmunds financed the $6,000 needed for the construction of the *Tourist*. Edmunds, C. G. Ridout, and Clara Ridout were the incorporators of the Tourist Company that had the mail contract for Lake Chelan. The company hired George C. Walker, a marine architect from Chicago, to supervise construction of the boat. The builders launched the *Tourist* on Thursday, June 14, and her trial trip followed the next Tuesday.

The new steamer was sixty-four feet long, eleven feet wide, and had a draft of four feet. A 100 horsepower fore and aft compound condensing engine (made in Chicago) powered by steam from a Scotch Marine Boiler propelled the boat. The single screw craft was one of the faster vessels then operating on the lake, traveling about twelve miles per hour. A crew of three usually manned the boat. Her first captain was Roy Smith, with E. L. Ward serving as engineer, and S. M. Campbell acting as purser. Later, Roy Barton (1907 to 1912), Robert Little, Willard Van Meter, and Ed Merritt served as captains. While Little performed as captain his engineer was Jack C. Enlow. Other crew members included Cliff Hendricks, Ted Pasley, and Lou Ward.

The *Tourist's* owners used the vessel to carry passengers, mail, and smaller sized general freight up lake two or three times a week. At the end of June in 1906 the boat took its first load of excursionists up lake to a dance at the Sunshine Hall where the Chelan Mandolin Orchestra entertained the group. The fare was only twenty-five cents for the night of revelry. More mundane tasks for the *Tourist* included pulling barge loads of horses, towing rafts of logs for the Pennell & Garton Sawmill, hauling apples for up lake growers, and transporting blasting powder and dynamite up lake to the mining camps.

The Boats, 1900-1906

Amos Edmunds supervising the construction of the Tourist

In her first year of operation the only known commercial boating fatality occurred on the lake in September. The *Tourist* was on her down lake run opposite Safety Harbor when Captain Roy Smith heard an outcry. When Smith looked behind the boat he saw someone struggling in the water and immediately signaled all stop. When there was no response the captain discovered that the engineer, Cliff Hendricks, was missing. The engineer had disappeared under the water before Smith could get the *Tourist* turned around. The *Lady of the Lake* came upon the scene and took on the *Tourist's* passengers and mail, and loaned her an engineer so that the latter could continue the search. The crew members found no trace of the unlucky engineer. The *Tourist* returned to the site of the accident the next day with Hendricks' brother, Joseph, to search the area again. They used grappling hooks and dynamite to try and raise the body, but were unsuccessful. The body was never recovered.

Richard Hulseman, who lived near Twenty Five Mile Creek, remembered riding the *Tourist* down lake with his family for the Fourth of July festivities in Chelan as a young boy. They would stay at the twenty-one room Tourist Hotel run by his aunt and uncle, Maria and William Ellingworth. His aunt was one of the first white women born in Washington Territory and his uncle was a former Indian scout. The celebrations lasted about three days and

Ladies of the Lake

Tourist, the U.S. mail boat

included horse racing and baseball games. Hulseman's fondest memory of these times was the encampment of Indians who set up their teepees near the race track, then located east of Chelan near the present dam. According to Hulseman, the Indians always brought their best horses and won most of the races.

An interesting trip involving the *Tourist* was described by Thomas E. Dodge, a Chelan Valley pioneer who settled at Twenty Five Mile Creek. Dodge was traveling from Rochester, New York to his new Chelan Valley home. After taking the train to Chicago he boarded one of the Great Northern Railway's "Tourist Sleepers" for the trip to Wenatchee. After spending the night he left on a paddle wheeled riverboat at daybreak for his journey from Wenatchee to Chelan Falls. At the rapids near present day Rocky Reach Dam the vessel had to use its steam capstan and cable to get the boat through. The riverboat reached Chelan Falls at five o'clock in the afternoon and from there Dodge took an open stage pulled by six horses up the steep grade and on to Campbell's Hotel Chelan. He spent a restful evening and the next morning he boarded the *Tourist*, captained by Roy Barton, for the trip to Twenty Five Mile Creek. The beauty of the Chelan Valley, especially the grandeur up lake from his destination, awed Dodge.

Like many of the boats the *Tourist* had its share of problems. In one incident, occurring in May of 1911, the vessel's tarp flew off in heavy winds near Twenty Five Mile Creek. The tarp got entangled in the boat's rudder and propeller causing the engine to stall. The *Tourist* drifted helplessly down lake

The Boats, 1900-1906

This 1910 photo shows Roy Barton at the helm of the Tourist with M. E. Field and his son, Hal; the men below include, C. G. Ridout, Bert Huey, Henry Cave, and a workman from Twenty Five Mile Creek

Ladies of the Lake

Tourist brings home a bear hunting party from up lake; on the top deck, from left to right, Mrs. Lloyd Pershall, Mrs. Clara Ridout, Lloyd Pershall, Scott M. Brown, Amos Edmunds, Steve Drew, and Al Pershall; the man in the lower window is Blaine Shepherd

for quite a distance until the crew finally got the tarp free and the engine restarted. A couple of years later a squall struck the *Tourist* near Green's Landing ripping the roof off the stern deck. The crew had to take the boat into the landing until the freak weather subsided.

    In 1915 Amos Edmunds sold the *Tourist* to Captain E. E. Shotwell of the Lake Chelan Transportation Company. Shotwell's boat company used the steamer to haul wood. Later the boat's owners used her for a short while as a fishing boat. It is not known when the *Tourist* was taken out of service, but it was possibly sometime around 1916. She was still in use in March of that year teaming with the *Comet* to push a barge to keep a channel into the Lakeside docks clear of ice.

Section Three

• • • • • • •

The Boats, 1910-1922

"In time ... the boats all acquired a homemade air like the cabins and shacks of the hills around."
Grant McConnell — Stehekin, A Valley in Time

Comet, 1910

In the spring of 1909 George E. Cottrell and the Tuttle family established the Lake Chelan Boat Company and it quickly became the area's premier boat building business. The Tuttles came to the Chelan Valley from Lake Washington where the patriarch of the family, Bailey J. Tuttle, had built and operated boats. The elder Tuttle was commonly referred to simply as "B.J." His sons, Chester and Thomas Tuttle, also ran the Lake View Hotel which they purchased from Joe Darnell that year. Chester had previously owned the Ives Hotel in Pateros. Sons Gaines and Fred, nicknamed "Cap," worked at the boat company with their father and brothers.

George Cottrell, by then a respected Lakeside boat builder, also constructed many of the rowboats in use on the lake at the time. Cottrell liked to race the launches he built against other boats on the lake. A much ballyhooed race between Cottrell's gasoline powered *Ona* and W. B. Lakely's *Corona* ended in an easy victory for the *Ona*. Besides his boat construction, Cottrell had the distinction of owning the first automobile in Lakeside. His car's air cooled engine was mounted in the back and he drove it using a boat-like tiller. Within two years Cottrell would sell his share of the boat company to the Tuttles and then move his family to Somers, Montana.

Ladies of the Lake

The Comet with B. J. Tuttle standing on the bow

In July of 1910 Cottrell and Tuttles' Lake Chelan Boat Company completed the *Comet* at their Lakeside boatyard. At the time the boat company had the Lake Chelan mail contract and needed a boat for that purpose. Tuttle designed boats were usually narrow with a pointed rear end just like the bow and the *Comet* was no exception to this design. The craft was the first gasoline powered boat to carry mail on Lake Chelan. A two cycle, two cylinder, twenty horsepower Strauble engine powered the *Comet*. The vessel was forty-two feet long and eight and one-half feet wide. That year the boat builders also built a thirty foot long gasoline powered boat called the *Rena*.

The *Comet's* first crew consisted of Captain B. J. Tuttle, with his son, Fred, acting as engineer. Claude W. Southwick worked as a deckhand on the boat. Jack Pasley, a former stage driver, was also employed by the company to work on the *Comet*. The vessel's first trip to Stehekin at the beginning of July was a success. The *Comet* covered the distance to the head of the lake in five and one-half hours, including twenty stops. Later, Captains Roy Barton, Lawrence Kingman and Robert Little piloted the *Comet*. Other crew members included Lyle Van Meter as engineer, Bert Huey, and Chauncey Van Meter.

In his book, *Stehekin, A Valley in Time*, Grant McConnell wrote that the Tuttles were not your conventional businessmen. The Tuttles rarely weighed the freight before they had it loaded aboard their boats. Consequently there were often disputes when those receiving the goods up lake did not agree to the assigned weight and resulting freight charges. Usually these matters got worked out when the Tuttles met with the aggrieved party and agreed that they had mistakenly overcharged the customer. One time a man had not received a large pump and asked if the Tuttles had seen it. They shook their heads, so the man contacted the railroad carrier who provided him with a receipt the Tuttles had signed for the pump. Armed with this bit of evidence, the man then confronted the Tuttles at their boatyard located near the site of the present day Caravel Resort. The Tuttle brothers looked at the receipt and started laughing. They admitted that the pump had fallen off the dock, unretrievably into the mud. The still grinning Tuttles paid the now speechless man the full value for his pump.

In 1912 the Tuttles sold both the *Comet* and *Rena* to the Lake Chelan Transportation Company which continued the *Comet* on the mail run and for general service. Ernest Pershall captained the boat for the transportation company, Fred "Cap" Tuttle acted as the engineer, and Willard Van Meter served as deckhand. When Willard later resigned from the company to attend school Clyde Varney took his place.

In February of 1913 the *Comet* encountered ice on her down lake mail run from Stehekin. Lake Chelan had frozen two inches thick from First Creek to Willow Point. The crew of the mail boat had to tie her up at Green's Landing and took the up lake mail from there the next morning. That day the *Comet* encountered ice one-half inch thick from Mountain Park to Granite Falls. The *Leader* commented that the last time the ice was so bad on the lake was during the winter of 1892-93 when the lake froze from Lakeside to near Willow Point.

In 1914 Richard Hulseman joined the *Comet's* crew as deckhand when he was only fourteen years old. He later recalled that the boat was not too seaworthy. Hulseman said that the front deck stuck out over the hull and when the boat encountered a large wave its deck would open like "an alligator's mouth." After the water rushed in, it was his job to use a hand pump to quickly clear water from the hull.

The mail run to Stehekin took an entire day, with the *Comet* returning to Lakeside the following day. While in Stehekin the crew usually slept on board, but took their meals at the Field Hotel. During her time on the lake the *Comet* performed many duties besides delivering the mail. Some of these chores included: transporting apples for growers in the Twenty Five Mile Creek area, towing telephone poles down from the head of the lake, taking hay up lake, and hauling barges of horses.

Around 1919 the Lake Chelan Transportation Company sold the *Comet* to Joe O'Neil. He usually used the boat to tow logs down from the head of the lake. The Warren Brothers were still using the boat in 1924 after C. C. Lafferty installed a new forty horsepower engine. Eventually Ed Hall owned the *Comet*, which he renamed the *Tramp*. In February of 1929 the *Leader* reported that Hall had taken out the boat's machinery and junked her hull.

Ladies of the Lake

Lena, 1913

In 1913 the Tuttles' Lake Chelan Boat Company built the *Lena* for Sherman Bell of Manson. The boat was thirty-three feet long and six feet wide. A seven horsepower, two cycle, Strauble gasoline engine propelled the craft along at a top speed of about ten miles per hour.

Bell's first job for the *Lena* was to haul lumber and other building materials from Lakeside for a new house he was building in Manson. At the time there was no road around Rocky Point so it was easier to bring in supplies by boat. Later Bell mainly used the craft as a pleasure boat, but he sometimes hired it out. According to Virginia Broden, Bell's granddaughter, he operated the boat commercially to earn money until his newly planted orchard came into production. Bell would also use the *Lena* to take his friends, such as Bill Phillips and Leslie McCown, on fishing excursions up lake.

Sherman Bell's daughter used the *Lena* to take her friends to dances and other social affairs in Chelan. After one St. Patrick's Day dance the group encountered ice in the lake making the return trip to Manson difficult. Luckily a friend came to their rescue in a more powerful steam powered boat and blazed a trail through the ice so that the *Lena* and her passengers could get home. The *Lena* eventually met a disastrous end when she hit some rocks near the Manson dock, ripping a hole in her bow and sinking the boat.

Manson to First Creek Ferry - the Chief, 1914

In the fall of 1913 members of both the First Creek and Manson Improvement Clubs lobbied the Chelan County commissioners to put a ferry in place between First Creek and Manson. At the time there was no road along the south shore and the apple growers in the First Creek area wanted the ferry to get their crop to market. The commissioners appropriated $2,000 of the ferry's expected cost of $2,400 and required that the additional money come from local funds. The county also stipulated that local funds be used to maintain the ferry. The two improvement clubs formed a stock company, the Manson-First Creek Ferry Association, to sell $1,300 worth of stock for this purpose. Leonard Olive, C. C. Ward, H. M. Thomas, and J. C. Gordon were appointed directors of this company.

Chelan County let bids for the new ferry in the spring of 1914. The Tuttles' Lake Chelan Boat Company won the contract to build the ferry. That summer the boat company built the fifty-six by twenty-two foot ferry. A twenty horsepower, four cycle, gas engine was to power the ferry on its estimated

The Boats, 1910-1922

Manson to First Creek Ferry, Charles Bell is on the right

fifteen minute crossing. The finished ferry would be large enough to hold four wagons with double teams or six automobiles when fully loaded. The Tuttles delivered the completed ferry to the Manson dock on July 14, 1914.

The new ferry, named the *Chief*, began operating in the last part of July after temporary docking facilities were in place at First Creek. Charles Bell and Jack Elliot ran the ferry which carried passengers, building supplies, and that season's First Creek apple crop. The county set the maximum allowable fares for the new trans-lake crossing at $1.00 for an automobile and $.75 for a double team and wagon. There were lesser charges for foot passengers and horses.

The *Chief's* first passenger trip was on July 30, when the ferry took seventy-five people from the Manson Union Sunday School to a picnic at First Creek. That fall the ferry hauled the First Creek apple crop and the lumber for Manson's new school. The following May, J. C. Gordon's First Creek sawmill sent over a load of lumber for Fred Phillips' Manson home. Later that summer Wenatchee residents discovered the ferry for use on their weekend automobile excursions.

Larue Barkley wrote that when his father, George, first came to the Chelan Valley in 1915 he took the ferry to Manson. It was at the top of Navarre Coulee on his way to the ferry at First Creek where George picked out his future orchard site. According to Larue his father selected the site because it was the only one that had a big pine tree at the top and another at the bottom.

Ladies of the Lake

In March of 1916 Charles Bell used the *Chief* to transport the up lake mail from below Willow Point to Green's Landing because ice prevented the *Comet* from doing so. The *Comanche* then picked up the mail from there. In April Bell took the *Chief* to be overhauled at Charley Lafferty's boatyard in Lakeside. The ferry never operated again after that because of the completion of the South Shore Road in June. Bell later took a job working for the water company in Manson. In March of 1918 the Chelan County commissioners sold the *Chief* back to the Lake Chelan Boat Company. Two years later the Tuttles sold the ferry to Charley Lafferty who used it as a barge.

In 1927 M. E. Field used the *Comanche* along with a barge as a Manson-First Creek ferry when the South Shore Road had to be moved in anticipation of the Chelan Dam raising the lake level. The Chelan Electrical Company agreed to finance the free ferry from September until December 1 of that year. Jack Wilson and V. T. Boaz, Jr. operated the ferry for Mr. Field. The ferry, mainly used to haul apples, could carry eight fully loaded trucks at a time. The ferry ran six days a week (excluding Sunday) and made five crossings per day.

May Bell / Princess, 1914

Captain Burley originally built the *Princess*, then named the *May Bell*, around 1911 for use on Lake Coeur d'Alene in Idaho. In 1914 Burley brought the boat to Lake Chelan and used it in conjunction with the Lake Chelan Navigation Company's boats to provide express service between Lakeside and Stehekin. That summer the *May Bell*, powered by a fifty horsepower gasoline engine, broke a Lake Chelan record by making two round-trips to Stehekin in one day.

In May of 1917 Captain Burley completed a remodel of the *May Bell*. The newly remodeled boat, renamed the *Princess*, was thirty-five feet long, had a narrow six foot width, and drew only two and one-half feet of water. After a trial run with the boat, Burley told the *Leader* that the *Princess* had not lost any of her former speed. Burley operated the *Princess* until August of 1920 when he sold it along with his Lakeside shop and boathouse to the Chelan Transfer Company. Crooker Perry operated the *Princess* for several years and then sold the boat to the Tuttles' Lake Chelan Boat Company.

In 1926, after Aaron Moore and Dave Harris had bought the Lake Chelan Boat Company from the Tuttles, they overhauled the *Princess*. During this time the boat was possibly extended to the craft's eventual length of fifty-five feet. The overhaul included the installation of a 150 horsepower Redwing gasoline engine that powered the boat to speeds of sixteen to eighteen miles per hour. At

Princess of Lake Chelan, "Finest and Fastest"

the time people considered her to be the "finest and fastest" passenger boat on Lake Chelan. However, riders on the *Princess* said that in rough water it was quite an experience as she tended to twist and turn so much that passengers in the back could see the front of the boat bending from one side to the other.

In February of 1929 the Lake Chelan Boat Company removed the *Princess's* engine and installed it in the *Liberty*. The following month high winds caused the *Princess* to be torn loose from her moorings. The motorless craft ended up on the beach by the boat company's dock, and luckily she sustained no damage. In April the company overhauled the *Princess* by putting in another engine and a new line shaft. Workers also scraped the hull and painted the entire vessel to get it ready for the season. The boat company operated the *Princess* for several more seasons, but the *Mirror* did not list it as one of the company's boats passing a state inspection in May of 1934.

By April of 1937 Fred Tuttle had acquired ownership of the *Princess*. Tuttle, who had started working at Grand Coulee Dam the year before, was one of the principal owners of a transportation company he had formed. He remodeled the *Princess* for use as a tour boat on the lake created behind the dam (later known as Lake Roosevelt). It is unknown how long the *Princess* operated on Lake Roosevelt.

Ladies of the Lake

Spokane, 1915

The Tuttles built the *Spokane* in 1915 at their new Chelan boatyard, located about where the present day Forest Service buildings are located. It was a trademark Tuttle boat — long and narrow. F. J. Potter, owner of Chelan's Ruby Theater, designed the boat for the Tuttles. Potter had a reputation for being a rather brilliant if not eccentric man and had worked on boats before coming to Chelan. As an interesting sidelight, several years later Potter and his wife, Cary, and stepdaughter, Ruby, moved to Vantage, Washington where he ran a ferry across the Columbia River. It was here that Potter shot his wife and threatened to shoot Ruby as she begged for her life. As Ruby pleaded, Potter relented and returned to his dead wife's side where he committed suicide. Ruby later told authorities that Potter had been assaulting her ever since the family had come to Chelan to operate the theater.

The *Spokane's* design may have been the work of a madman, but it proved to be successful. The boat was seventy feet long and ten feet, eight inches wide and weighed seven and one-half tons. The boat's design called for a 150 horsepower gasoline engine, but initially the Tuttles used a forty-two

Picture showing the narrow design of the Spokane

The Boats, 1910-1922

The Spokane, designed by a former owner of the Ruby Theater

horsepower Strauble motor from their forty-five foot launch called the *Panama* (built in 1914). This gasoline engine powered a single screw that propelled the vessel at a speed of eleven and one-half miles per hour. The *Spokane's* main cabin could seat forty-eight people, the smoking room accommodated sixteen, a deckhouse had room for eight, and there was outside seating on the top sides of the cabin for twenty-five. The main cabin had steel framed veneer seats that faced forward with armrests that were level with the bottom of the windows for maximum visibility for the passengers.

The Tuttles held a "name the boat" contest and L. N. Pershall came up with the name for the *Spokane*. With a large gathering of people, the builders launched the new boat at the Chelan dock the end of May. The *Spokane's* maiden voyage to the head of the lake occurred on Wednesday, June 9, 1915. On the following Sunday the boat started its regular run to Stehekin with the Chelan Band on board to entertain the passengers. That summer, from the middle of June to the middle of September, the *Spokane* traveled 12,000 miles on the lake and carried 2,500 passengers. The Tuttles happily reported that through it all their new boat worked without a single mishap.

The next summer the *Spokane* had much the same success. To entice even more business, the Tuttles offered special Stehekin excursion rates for the first two weeks in July. The excursion boat left Chelan at 7:00 a.m. and returned

Ladies of the Lake

at 6:30 p.m. for a fare of $2.00 — children were one-half price. With business booming the Tuttles decided to upgrade the *Spokane's* engine. That winter they installed a new 150 horsepower, eight cylinder, four cycle Sterling gasoline engine. At full speed the engine turned 1,000 revolutions per minute.

In April of 1917 the Tuttles invited some townspeople to be their guests on the *Spokane's* first of the season head of the lake excursion. That day the boat's crewmen were Captain Gaines Tuttle, Fred Tuttle as engineer, and Chester Tuttle as purser. Among those making the trip were: Mr. and Mrs. F. J. Potter and daughter (Ruby), Mr. and Mrs. W. E. Rubottom and son, Mr. and Mrs. O. A. Hoag, Mrs. Jennie Sleigh, Mrs. Chester A. Tuttle and baby, Mrs. C. C. Campbell, Mr. and Mrs. E. H. McDaniels and child, Mrs. C. Rubin and daughter, Mrs. Bailey J. Tuttle and daughter, Sam Long, Fred Merritt, C. W. Hall, Tom Jett, Dr. G. W. Moore, Mrs. Fred F. Tuttle, and J. Yotter. The trip was a success and the boat's sixteen mile per hour speed, provided by the larger engine, impressed everyone.

In May of 1917 the graduating class of Chelan High School chartered the *Spokane* for its end of the year excursion to Stehekin. The boat, captained by Gaines Tuttle, left Lakeside and arrived at the head of the lake three and one-half hours later. Once there the group scattered in many directions with some of the class members content to lounge in and around the Field Hotel. At 3:00 p.m. a torrential downpour forced the entire party to return to the hotel to seek sanctuary and dry out. Soon they all boarded the *Spokane* for the festive return trip. While heading home two male class members sang a duet from "Die Wacht am Rhein," and later others good-naturedly roasted one of their teachers, Professor A. T. Sutton. After the *Spokane* docked at Lakeside the students thanked Tuttle for the pleasant journey.

It is not known when the *Spokane* was taken out of service on Lake Chelan, but the *Leader* reported that the boat was still operating — hauling apples — in November of 1921. Besides the *Spokane* the Tuttles built several other commercial boats including the tug *Vagabond*, and a passenger boat called the *Panama*. In 1920 the Tuttles sold the *Panama* to R. M. Accord of Bridgeport, Washington. Accord used the boat to push a freight barge on the Columbia River. They also built several smaller boats for private individuals such as the *Moore*, and the *Copper Queen*. The Tuttles built another larger boat, approximately sixty-four feet long, that they shipped to Coeur d'Alene, Idaho. That boat was still in operation in the early 1960s being used to push a sightseeing barge.

The Boats, 1910-1922

Comanche, 1915

In 1915 the Lake Chelan Transportation Company, then run by E. E. Shotwell and Roy Barton, completed construction of the *Comanche*. The company built the boat on the beach near George Cottrell's old boat works. The craft's shipbuilding crew consisted of Bill Tinnie, Lyle Van Meter, Willard Van Meter, Bert Huey, and Knute Hjelvik. Shotwell also hired a master boat builder from Everett, named A. J. Goulette, to supervise the project. With little fanfare the transportation company launched the boat on May 14 and made a short maiden voyage just off the Lakeside dock on May 22. The following day she made a longer run to First Creek and back. The *Comanche's* first regular run to Stehekin was on June 7.

The *Comanche* was seventy-six feet long, had a beam of fourteen feet eight inches, and a draft of four feet. Her original engine was a heavy duty, ninety horsepower, three cylinder, Imperial gasoline engine that gave the boat a twelve mile per hour cruising speed. Later the *Comanche's* owners upgraded her engine to a 150 horsepower Hall Scott. The *Comanche* was the first large gasoline powered commercial boat on Lake Chelan. The craft was capable of carrying ninety passengers on her upper deck and up to four automobiles or livestock and freight on the lower deck. A stairway amidships provided access to the upper cabin and pilothouse. Roy Barton often captained the boat with John Rainier acting as the engineer. Ray Culver also worked on the vessel.

North Central Washington Museum, Wenatchee, WA

The Comanche after her conversion to a freight boat

Ladies of the Lake

The Lake Chelan Transportation Company used the *Comanche* to push a barge that the company had A. J. Goulette build for them to haul sheep. The boat company had the barge built when the region's sheepmen had to find another range for their sheep after the Forest Service closed the upper Methow to grazing because it became too populated. At a December 1915 meeting in North Yakima (attended by the sheepmen, officials of the Forest Service, and representatives of the transportation company) the participants agreed to build the barge with the sheepmen contributing $2,500 for its construction. When completed in the spring of 1916 the barge was ninety feet long, twenty feet wide, and had a draft of six and one-half feet. Named the *Blackfoot*, her three decks could hold 2,400 sheep. The barge took its first load of sheep from Lakeside to Prince Creek on May 28. One year the barge hauled 63,000 sheep to and from the head of the lake.

Tom Drumheller, at the time a prominent sheepman, used the *Comanche* and the *Blackfoot* barge to move his sheep. Drumheller wintered his livestock near Ephrata and in the spring herded the sheep toward Lake Chelan. Their route took them down Brown's Canyon and to the Columbia River across from Chelan Falls where the herders ferried the animals across. From there Drumheller drove his herds to Lakeside where they boarded the *Blackfoot* for the trip up lake. The sheep summered on the Chelan-Methow ridge in what was then called the Chelan National Forest. In July Drumheller would round up the fatter lambs

Tom Drumheller's sheep being loaded on the Blackfoot at Lakeside; Crooker Perry's private launch is on the left

The Boats, 1910-1922

and barge them down lake. The herders then loaded the sheep on railroad cars at Chelan Falls for the trip to Chicago. When Drumheller's Lake Chelan sheep operation was at its peak he was shipping seventy railroad cars of sheep to Chicago annually.

When not pushing the sheep barge the *Comanche* still functioned as a passenger and charter boat. Chelan High School often chartered the boat for up lake outings. One day in May of 1916 students and faculty of the high school boarded the craft at 7:30 a.m. for the trip to Stehekin. At 11:30 a.m. the hungry group had lunch on board just before landing. Once docked they hiked their way to Rainbow Falls. The *Leader* reported that Myrton Crow, Marshall Brown, and George Pennell hustled to be the first to get to the falls. After an adventuresome outing the high schoolers reboarded the *Comanche* at 3:30 p.m. for the journey home, arriving at Lakeside at 8:45 p.m.

For the next three years the *Comanche* was a workhorse for the Lake Chelan Transportation Company. The following are just a few of the tasks she performed during that period: the boat and barge hauled a load of corn to M. E. Field's place at Deer Point, took a herd of fourteen cattle up lake to the K. B. Wuelfinger place, transported fifteen horses to Lucerne for Oscar Getty, freighted five horses to Grade Creek for the Forest Service to use to pack in supplies for a 1917 forest fire, and hauled countless boxes of apples for up lake growers. One of the more unusual jobs in 1918 had the *Comanche* pushing the barge up lake loaded with an old dismantled house that the Forest Service planned to use as a fire lookout on Stormy Mountain. Near the end of her service for the company, the *Comanche* ferried tourists and their cars up lake to Stehekin. Of course, through it all, the barge continued to haul sheep.

In January of 1920 Crooker Perry of Lakeside bought the *Comanche* and the *Blackfoot* for use in his passenger and freight business called the Perry Boat Company. On September 16, 1921 the boat and barge were heading down lake loaded with 1,200 sheep when it was involved in a spectacular accident. Roy Barton was on board, but another man was piloting the *Comanche* when the *Blackfoot* hit a barely submerged rock about a mile up from the site of the present day Yacht Club. Barton and the other man quickly cut the barge free from the boat and then pushed the sinking barge into Rock Haven Bay. There the men moved many of the sheep to a small peninsula, but 400 to 500 of the panicked animals on the barge's lower deck drowned. Barton later said that the Perry Boat Company paid the sheep's owner, Morrow Brothers of Sunnyside, a "couple thousand dollars," as they were "pretty cheap then." After the accident the crew towed the damaged barge back to Lakeside for repairs. Until the boat company repaired the barge Tom Drumheller was forced to herd his sheep from Ephrata to Pateros where he ferried the animals across the Columbia River to continue up the Methow Valley to their summer range.

Ladies of the Lake

In 1921 Cooker Perry almost started a fare war on the lake when his boat company petitioned the Washington State Department of Public Works to lower the round-trip passenger fare to Stehekin from $4.50 to $2.50. This drew an immediate protest from the Tuttles and their Lake Chelan Boat Company that the fare was too low and not profitable. After protracted legal haggling the Department of Public Works allowed the Perry Boat Company to charge a $3.50 fare because the department ruled that the *Comanche* was not as fast or up-to-date as the Tuttles' boats. Freight rates on the lake were to remain the same for all boat companies operating on the lake. The rift between the Perry and the Lake Chelan boat companies heated up after Perry paid the Chelan Band to play on the *Comanche* for its Fourth of July excursion. Chelan people chastised the band members for not supporting "home institutions." The criticism forced the band secretary, Warren Harris, to write a letter to the *Leader* expressing the band's appreciation to the Tuttles for allowing them to play on the *Cascade Flyer* in June when it made its initial Stehekin cruise. The feud also reflected the growing resentment between the communities of Chelan and Lakeside over which town would control the lower end of the lake.

In September of 1925 Crooker Perry sold the *Comanche* and the *Blackfoot* barge to M. E. Field for $1,500. The next year Field had the *Comanche* overhauled and by May the boat was back in action taking Dan Devore's pack horses back up lake. In June Field began a contract with the Grant Smith Construction Company, builders of the Chelan Dam, to use the *Comanche* and

The Chelan Dam under construction

The Boats, 1910-1922

the *Blackfoot* to help clear the shoreline at the head of the lake to the 1100 foot level. In addition they also hauled equipment for the company. During this work Marion Parrish piloted the *Comanche* and Dillon Henderson served as her engineer. The *Comanche* towed some of the timber from the 500 acres cleared up lake to be used as pilings in the construction of the new dam.

In the early part of 1927 the *Comanche* and the *Blackfoot* barge continued hauling supplies for the Grant Smith Construction Company. After the Chelan Dam's first generator began operating on September 1 the *Comanche* and the barge returned to hauling mixed freight, apples, and sheep. As mentioned earlier, the boat and barge temporarily served as a Manson to First Creek ferry from mid-September to December 1. Starting in January of 1928 the *Comanche* and *Blackfoot* were moving houses still below the 1100 foot lake level, as that would be the first year that the dam would raise the lake to that height. M. E. Field and his son, Hal, first moved a house at Elephant Rock and then transported a home owned by Dr. T. Congdon from Lightning Creek to Shrine Beach.

That spring Field and his son had the barge stripped of her decks, and put on wooden sidewalks and a roof that covered a newly installed smooth dance floor. Hal Field then operated the barge as a floating dance hall, towing the barge with one of his larger power boats mainly between Chelan and Manson. The first dance on the barge followed the Lake Chelan Apple Blossom Day parade held in Manson on May 4. The dance barge took seventy-five couples at a time out on the lake, returning several times to the Manson dock for other couples as the dancing continued into the evening.

Chelan Dam spilling water in 1928

Ladies of the Lake

In August Hal Field towed the dance barge to Stehekin for a Tuesday evening dance. Young people from Chelan, not wanting to miss a good dancing opportunity, chartered the *Princess* to the head of the lake to attend the dance. Among those making the trip were: Marie Hair, Ruth Renn, Ada Emerson, Evelyn Hanks, Alice Mae Russell, Wilma Dexter, Estelle Pease, Henrietta Kelsey, Pauline Shipton, Claude Bennett, Thomas Holleque, James Reed, Dr. W. S. Kelsey, Modest Peters, Harold Bragg, Ralph Meenach, Dale Copeland, Walter Morris, Paul Sparks, and Kenneth Hargett. The *Chelan Valley Mirror* reported that the group had quite a good time, and returned home at 4:30 a.m. the next day.

In 1930 the Field's sold the *Comanche* to Dave F. Harris, owner of the Lake Chelan Boat Company. The boat company mainly used the vessel as their freight boat, but it did carry passengers as well. The craft hauled in many of the supplies for the Howe Sound Mining Company's Holden Mine operations. In January of 1938 an early evening fire ravaged the *Comanche* as she sat at the Lakeside dock. The fire started in the "Delco room," and quickly spread to badly burn the engine compartment and the rear of the cabin. The blaze did not damage the hull and the boat company made repairs and soon had the *Comanche* back on her regular run. In April she was one of the many boats which escorted the new Howe Sound tug, the *E. B. Schley*, down lake as the tug towed her first load of Holden Mine ore concentrate from Lucerne to Chelan.

Howe Sound crane at Lucerne which was used to try and lift the Comanche for repairs

The Boats, 1910-1922

The boat company continued to operate the vessel until 1945, when a minor accident at Stehekin started a series of events that ended the boat's long service on Lake Chelan. Things started to go wrong for the *Comanche* when she missed the Stehekin Landing during an attempted night docking. After missing the dock the boat continued up lake toward the mouth of the Stehekin River where she hit a snag, damaging her propeller and rudder. The boat company had the *Comanche* towed to the Howe Sound Mining dock at Lucerne to attempt repairs. While the mining company's crane was lifting her stern out of the water the boat broke in two. Now totaled, the *Comanche's* owners dismantled her, salvaging her engine and accessories. They towed the boat's shell just down lake from Lightning Creek where they burned the boat to the hull and then sunk it. During low water one can still see her remains at what is now called Comanche Bay.

Mohawk, 1916

In the spring of 1916 the Lake Chelan Transportation Company built the *Mohawk*. An Everett boat building company fabricated her oak frames and then sent them to Lakeside where local workers laid the keel. When completed the *Mohawk* was sixty feet long, ten and one-half feet wide, and had a four foot draft. The boat had a freight capacity of approximately twenty-five tons. A 150 horsepower, four cycle, gasoline engine powered the craft to a top speed of eighteen miles per hour. A large crowd was present when the transportation company launched the $3,500 boat on Saturday, May 20. The company had built a barge at the same time and usually used it with the *Mohawk* to haul freight.

In January of 1920 Charley Lafferty bought the *Mohawk* and the old Manson-First Creek ferry barge from the Lake Chelan Transportation Company. Lafferty used the boat and the barge to haul apples, horses, general freight, and as a pile driver. Lafferty later sold the *Mohawk* and barge to Garry Anderson, owner of the Mohawk Boat Company, who continued using them to haul freight. Early on the morning of August 2, 1921 a fire destroyed the *Mohawk* which Anderson had loaded with $800 worth of freight the night before. The disaster left only a charred hull.

After the fire Crooker Perry acquired the *Mohawk*. In March of 1925 he sold the hull to a cooperative of Twenty Five Mile Creek orchardists who planned to convert the hull into a barge. The growers in the cooperative were E. A. Smith, R. W. Barks, Frank Sharratt, M. E. Field, W. A. Young, and Carl Schweke. The group contracted with Claude W. Southwick and Marion Parrish to remodel the *Mohawk* into a barge without an engine. Southwick's boat, the

Ladies of the Lake

Early Chelan Valley apple harvest

The Boats, 1910-1922

Mohawk

Wanda, pushed the apple loaded barge. That fall Marion Parrish and his helper, W. S. White, used the boat and barge to transport 20,163 boxes of apples. Lake Chelan Fruit Growers shipped the majority of the fruit (10,863 boxes) along with the Beebe Fruit Growers which shipped E. A. Smith's crop of 9,300 boxes of apples.

In 1926 Hal Field bought the *Mohawk*. Field and Harry Hunt transported apples with the *Mohawk* barge using a smaller vessel called the *Charlotte Mary*. Later that year Field had Charley Lafferty install a 175 horsepower Sterling gasoline engine and rebuild her cabin. In 1927 Field used the boat to haul equipment and crews clearing the lakeshore in anticipation of the new dam raising the lake level. That fall the *Mohawk* also pushed barge loads of apples for up lake growers. The *Mohawk* later burned again when some spilled stove kerosene was accidentally ignited. The resulting fire scorched the boat, but she got underway that day.

In the 1930s the *Mohawk's* owners used her for chartered excursion groups and fishing parties. On one trip in May of 1935 the boat took seniors from Chelan High School on their "sneak" day. The seniors and their chaperones traveled to the Field's ranch, near Twenty Five Mile Creek, and boarded the *Mohawk* at 4:30 a.m. The boat's first stop, at 7:00 a.m., was at Prince Creek where the group had breakfast. Next the boat took the students to the Meadow Creek Lodge for a stop and then they were on their way to Stehekin. There the students hiked to a picnic area for lunch and then continued on to Rainbow

Ladies of the Lake

Meadow Creek Lodge

Falls. At 7:00 p.m. the seniors reboarded the *Mohawk* for a quick trip back to Meadow Creek Lodge where they had dinner and a dance. The *Mirror* reported that the group had a "grand time," but that it was very quiet on the early morning return trip as the students had classes that day.

Around 1940, salvagers dismantled the *Mohawk* at Lafferty's Boat Shop, near where Pat and Mike's store is presently located.

Wanda, early 1920s

Around 1923 Claude W. Southwick carved the *Wanda's* bow from a maple tree and used oak ribbing and cedar planking in the boat he built at Gold Creek. The clipper style vessel was thirty-six feet long. In 1925, when Southwick prepared the boat to push the *Mohawk* apple barge, he installed a Stevens-Durea forty-eight horsepower motor in the launch. Southwick's thirteen year old son, Claude R. Southwick, began serving as a deckhand on the boat during World War II when there was a shortage of men. Because laws prevented the elder Southwick from paying his son he charged himself enough overtime to cover his son's wages. Southwick later sold the *Wanda* to the Chelan Box and Manufacturing Company, and they may have shortened her by six feet because of hull damage. The box company used the boat to haul logs and replaced it in 1957 or 1958 with another boat.

The Boats, 1910-1922

Liberty, 1918

Tom Tuttle of the Lake Chelan Boat Company built the *Liberty* during the winter of 1917-18. The boat's name referred to the Liberty War Bond drive that was then underway to help finance the United States' World War I expenditures. When completed in the spring of 1918 the *Liberty* was forty-five feet long and nine feet wide. A six cylinder, 150 horsepower Sterling gasoline engine powered the boat.

Chester Tuttle captained the *Liberty* which the company built to be used as a mail boat. The company also used it as a winter boat and for charters. At various times the Tuttles used the *Liberty* to push barges and to make special trips. One of these trips occurred in June of 1922 when the boat took twenty men and supplies to help fight a 1,000 acre forest fire below Little Big Creek.

In June of 1927 the Tuttles sold the *Liberty* and the Lake Chelan Boat Company to Aaron Moore and Dave Harris. The men used the *Liberty* as a replacement for the *Tenino*, a thirty-seven foot launch which was the first boat Moore and Harris owned on the lake. They later traded the *Tenino* for a new engine for the *Cascade Flyer*. In 1929 the boat company took the 150 horsepower Redwing gasoline engine from the *Princess* and installed it in the *Liberty*.

One day in February of 1930 Aaron Moore was painfully burned in a fire aboard the *Liberty*. Moore was working in the bow of the boat and could not find the light switch so he struck a match. The spark caused gasoline fumes in the bow to explode. With his clothes on fire, Moore dashed up on deck and

Liberty coming into dock

jumped into the lake saving himself. The resulting fire burned the engine room and pilothouse. The boat company quickly repaired the damage and the *Liberty* was soon back in service.

The *Liberty* performed various jobs for the Lake Chelan Boat Company over the next seven years. For one task in 1934 the Washington Water Power Company chartered the vessel to put out buoys by rocky points along the lake to enhance navigation. In the spring of 1938 the boat company remodeled the aging craft. When finished the *Liberty* had new upholstered seats and a refurbished cabin that accommodated thirty-five passengers. Workers also attractively painted the boat to get it ready for the season. The boat company planned to use the *Liberty* as a replacement boat when they later overhauled both the *Cascade Flyer* and the *Speedway*.

On January 14, 1943, the *Liberty* partially sank when a big storm hit the Chelan Valley. The boat company had moored her next to the *Speedway*, whose motor A. L. Marcuson was repairing. Heavy wave action tore the *Liberty* loose from her moorings and tossed her about until she slammed into the Howe Sound Mining Company's dock submerging the stern of the boat. Although the *Speedway* remained tied up to the dock the waves crashed over her railings and she met a fate similar to the *Liberty's*. The boat company raised and repaired both boats and they were soon back in service.

In late November and early December of 1945 the *Liberty* carried the bodies of those drowned in a school bus accident to Chelan. Elton Dexter stayed at the scene with the boat for six days. The *E. B. Schley* and one of the Howe Sound's barges also played a significant role in the recovery operation.

In 1947 the Lake Chelan Boat Company replaced the *Liberty's* gasoline engine with a 165 horsepower GMC 6.71 diesel engine. With the new engine the boat cruised at approximately sixteen miles per hour. The company continued to use the boat for charters and for regular passenger runs. In 1957 her owners retired the *Liberty* because she was too expensive to maintain and considered no longer safe to operate. That year the boat company burned the *Liberty* on the beach near their present day docking facilities.

Victory, 1919

In 1919 the Tuttles launched the *Victory*, another boat with their trademark design — long and narrow. Her name celebrated the Allied triumph in World War I the previous November. The craft was sixty-three feet long, had a width of ten feet, and drew three and one-half feet of water. An eight cylinder, 150 horsepower Sterling gasoline engine powered the boat. Because the Tuttles installed the engine in the front of the boat it required a long propeller shaft.

Her owners used the *Victory*, which could carry about sixty people, to transport the mail, as a passenger boat, and for charters. Some of the *Victory's* charters included taking the Chelan Valley Republican Club to their annual meeting at Manson, touring a group of state newspaper editors up lake, and hosting the Wenatchee Apollo Club's annual up lake outing.

The *Victory* met a watery death on June 16, 1929 when she caught fire while on a fishing charter. The mishap occurred at the head of the lake about 300 feet below the painted rocks across from the Stehekin landing. The episode began after a carburetor backfire started the engine on fire. The blaze quickly enveloped the *Victory* causing the crew and passengers to abandon ship. While other boats in the area picked up the castaways the *Victory* burned to the water line and eventually sank in about ninety feet of water. The boat company estimated their loss on the boat to be $6,000 of which $3,500 was covered by insurance.

After the incident the *Wenatchee World* reported that the *Victory* did not have the required amount of safety equipment on board at the time of the accident. L. A. Moore of the Lake Chelan Boat Company disputed this saying that the state had inspected the boat a few days before the fire. Moore said that the company had equipped the vessel with four fire extinguishers and ninety life preservers — well above the legal limits.

Cascade Flyer, 1921

In 1921 Tuttle and Sons built the *Cascade Flyer*, and launched it on Sunday, May 15. She had a knife-like bow that widened to a maximum beam of nine feet, and had a three foot draft. A 300 horsepower Sterling gasoline engine powered the sixty-five foot passenger and mail boat. The vessel had seating for sixty-five passengers. The new boat cost the Tuttles approximately $11,000 to construct, but would allow them to double their passenger capacity. Chester Tuttle told the *Leader* that the Lake Chelan Boat Company had carried 4,000 passengers the previous season and now expected to improve on that number. Tuttle went on to say that their new boat would make daily trips to the head of the lake starting July 1. The craft would leave Chelan after the arrival of the afternoon train and reach Stehekin at 9:00 p.m. and return the next day so that travelers could make their train connections.

To build interest in the new boat the Tuttles arranged for the Wenatchee Rotary Club to select a name for the new boat. On Saturday, June 4, 1921, Ethel May and Winona Edwards, daughters of Mr. and Mrs. Ira Edwards, christened the boat by breaking a bottle of Wenatchee apple cider over the bow as they said, "I christen thee the Cascade Flyer." The boat's motor was then started and

Ladies of the Lake

the Rotary members and their families boarded the vessel for its inaugural trip to Stehekin. The Chelan Band went along to entertain the passengers with a variety of musical selections. The *Leader* reported that the *Cascade Flyer* made the trip from the Chelan dock to Stehekin in two hours and fifteen minutes which, supposedly, set a new lake record.

The *Cascade Flyer* did a good business her first year of operation. To prepare for the 1922 season the Tuttles put the boat into dry dock for an overhaul. The *Leader* reported in May that the work was done and the Tuttles had equipped the *Flyer* with a "380 horsepower Sterling engine of the same type used in U. S. sub chasers." The report went on to say that the engine gave the boat a rated top speed of 30 miles per hour and that a trip to the head of the lake would take only two and one-half hours. It is doubtful that the *Cascade Flyer's* engine was new, but her owners were no doubt correcting or inflating the size of the motor for promotional purposes.

In the following years the *Cascade Flyer* and the boat company's other boats continued to do well. After the summer season of 1926 the Tuttles claimed that approximately 300 people a week went up lake on their boats. They said that the boats averaged forty passengers per day on the weekdays, and sixty passengers on Sunday.

In June of 1927 Aaron Moore and Dave Harris acquired the *Cascade Flyer* when the pair bought the Lake Chelan Boat Company from the Tuttles (Harris, from St. Andrews, Washington, had been awarded the lake's mail

New Woodin Ave Bridge, built in 1927

The Boats, 1910-1922

Cascade Flyer off-loading passengers

contract the previous year and at first used the launch, *Scout*, to deliver the mail). In May of 1928 Moore and Harris traded their thirty-seven foot launch, the *Tenino*, to the Auto-Interurban Company of Spokane for a new engine for the *Flyer*. The Spokane company planned to use the *Tenino* on Lake Coeur d'Alene. The new power plant which the Lake Chelan Boat Company got in return was a 300 horsepower "Coast Guard" Sterling gasoline engine. Besides the *Flyer* the new owners of the boat company had two launches, the *Princess* and the *Whippet*, along with their other larger boats — the *Liberty* and the *Victory*. That year the company also launched a freight boat called the *Dragon*.

With the raising of the lake level in the spring of 1928 the city of Chelan tried to entice Moore and Harris to build their new dock in Chelan by offering to pay part of the cost. Instead the boat company built a freight dock at Lakeside, but they did complete a dock in Chelan the next spring. To save money they no longer took the mail or passengers up lake from the Lakeside dock, but transported them by car to the Twenty Five Mile Creek landing to be put on the boat there. The car left Lakeside at 7:00 a.m. and started its return from the landing at 9:30 a.m.

In the winter of 1928-29 the Lake Chelan Boat Company offered up lake excursions to try and increase their off-season business. In February of 1929 the *Cascade Flyer* took members of the Chelan and Wenatchee Rotary Clubs to Stehekin. One of the big draws for these cruises was an activity where the passengers counted the wildlife they saw along the shoreline as the boat made its way to the head of the lake. On this trip the Rotarians and their spouses saw 238 deer, forty-seven mountain goats, two coyotes, two ducks, one eagle, and one rabbit. Rotary members also put up a pot of money for the first woman to see a deer. The $1.76 jackpot was won by Mrs. H. B. Varney. The winter trips proved to be very successful and continued for many years.

In the spring of 1929 Moore and Harris incorporated the Lake Chelan Boat Company for $50,000. Moore served as president of the company, while Harris acted as secretary. They each held $15,000 in stock and offered the remaining $20,000 in stock to be sold at one dollar per share. It was a preferred stock offering that promised investors seven percent interest per year on their holdings. With the new capital the boat company planned to completely overhaul the *Liberty*, *Victory*, *Princess*, and *Cascade Flyer*. The overhaul for the *Flyer* that May included the installation of a 150 horsepower, six cylinder, Hall Scott gas engine. With the new engine the vessel could cruise at approximately sixteen miles per hour.

When the Howe Sound Mining operations at Holden began in the early 1930s the *Cascade Flyer* ran an alternating weekly schedule with another Lake Chelan Boat Company boat, the *Speedway*. The *Speedway* did the Stehekin run three days a week while the *Cascade Flyer* would run only as far as Lucerne on the alternating days. The *Flyer* continued in service until the company semi-retired the boat in the early 1940s, using her mainly as a freight boat.

Filming of the MGM motion picture, *Courage of Lassie* (starring Elizabeth Taylor), at various locations up lake in the fall of 1944 brought the *Cascade Flyer* back into more regular service. MGM also hired other boats — the *Myrju*, the *Wanda*, and the *Liberty* — to transport actors, animals, and equipment. The *Myrju* was H. W. Van Slyke's private cruiser that Charley Lafferty had built for him in 1929. The Lake Chelan Boat Company had not used the deteriorating *Cascade Flyer* for some time before they placed her back in service hauling freight and supplies up lake for MGM. One of the boat's biggest problems was a balky engine that needed constant attention to keep it running. This problem would lead to the *Flyer's* demise.

That fall the boat company had crammed the *Cascade Flyer* with a huge load of MGM's supplies and $800 worth of groceries. The crew operating the *Flyer* at the time was pilot, Claude Southwick, Sr., and deckhand, Ted Housden. The boat encountered a violent storm as she headed to the filming sites at Moore Point and Lucerne. The *Flyer* was just below Safety Harbor when a large wave swamped the craft blowing off the hatch cover. Water poured into the hatch and drowned out the engine. About the same time the violent action caused a large side of beef to blast through the bulkhead behind the cabin. As her crew furiously worked to restart the engine, heavy winds, both down lake and side gusts, buffeted the vessel. As the *Flyer* drifted aimlessly and sideways in the heavy swells her load suddenly shifted. In desperation Southwick yelled to Housden to throw all the remaining sides of beef off the top of the boat. However, heavy cases of canned goods kept the struggling craft listing so much to one side that the water was up to the windows. After working feverishly, but unsuccessfully, to correct the load Southwick and Housden started jettisoning the supplies. This righted the *Flyer* enough that she then drifted across the lake where she crashed stern first into large rocks just above Twenty Five Mile Creek. The *Flyer* then came around with her bow pointed down lake to be repeatedly dashed on the rocks wrecking her beyond repair. Luckily, both Southwick and Housden were able to safely jump off the boat onto the rocks without even getting wet.

The crew of the *Speedway* had seen that the *Cascade Flyer* was in trouble, but the severity of the storm forced her into Twenty Five Mile Creek for safe haven. For days after the accident people living on the lake near the creek found canned goods and other debris awash on the shoreline. Within a few days the Howe Sound Mining tug and barge recovered the *Flyer's* hull and hauled it to Lakeside where the barge's crane placed the remains on the beach. The boat company had the hull guarded for several days while expensive equipment that the *Flyer* had carried in her forward hold was accounted for. Afterwards the boat company salvaged the *Flyer* and then burned her hull on the beach.

Tuttle Barge, 1922

In September of 1922 the Tuttles' Lake Chelan Boat Company launched a freight barge they had built specifically to haul apples. The barge was sixty-four feet long and twelve feet wide and it had live rollers to facilitate the loading and unloading of fruit. A fifty horsepower engine powered a sternwheel that propelled the craft at about ten miles per hour. The barge had a capacity of thirty-five tons and could carry up to 1,500 boxes of apples.

Later that month the barge was heading down lake with a load of 400 boxes of apples from the Buckner orchard at Stehekin, 300 boxes from the E. A. Smith ranch at Twenty Five Mile Creek, and O. J. Hart's household goods when it ran into "heavy seas." A large wave washed over the barge and filled the hull with water. The crew immediately headed the barge to shore as the craft became halfway submerged in the water. The barge finally reached land where the crew quickly offloaded the cargo. The barge was not damaged, but there was about $300-$400 worth of damage to the household items.

Ladies of the Lake

Tragedy of another kind struck the Tuttle family in October when B. J. Tuttle was hit by a car in Lakeside. After lingering in a coma for eight days he finally died on October 20, 1922. The *Leader* noted that Tuttle and his four sons had been boat builders and operators on Lake Chelan since 1907 and that B. J. would always be remembered as "a quiet unassuming, kindly gentleman." His obituary said that Tuttle had been born in Kentucky in 1855 and came west by wagon train via the Green River route when he was twenty-three years old. He first settled near Uniontown, in Whitman County, to farm and then moved to Douglas County where he farmed 160 acres. He was survived by his wife, Juliza, and his six children — Tom, Fred, Gaines, Chester, Nina, and Mildred Brockman of Yakima. Tuttle's sons would sell the Lake Chelan Boat Company within five years of his death.

Section Four
••••••
The Boats, 1929-1998

"I guess you could say its being built by a farmer."
Larry Cozart, builder of the Lady of the Lake II

Speedway, 1929

In 1926 Charley Lafferty began construction of the single decked *Speedway* at his boatyard for the Lake Chelan Boat Company then co-owned by Dave F. Harris and Aaron Moore. When the boat company launched the *Speedway* in 1929 she was sixty-two feet long, had a twelve and one-half foot beam, and drew three and one-half feet of water. Two 200 horsepower Sterling gasoline engines shipped from Buffalo, New York initially powered the twin screw boat. The engines allowed the *Speedway* to cruise at top speeds of fifteen to seventeen miles per hour while carrying a load of seventy-five passengers. Each engine had cost the company $3,000 and the boat company estimated that they had from $13,000 to $14,000 invested in the boat. The company emphasized that the design of the new engines made them immune from backfiring, hoping to alleviate the public's concern after the *Victory's* fire and sinking in June of 1929.

During the summer of 1929 there was much excitement in anticipation of the new boat. The city of Chelan had recently installed a new public boat landing at Campbell's Hotel. This was a convenience not only for passengers, but for the town's merchants who regularly needed to load supplies on the boats for the up lake resorts.

Ladies of the Lake

The single-decked Speedway at Domke Falls

That fall Harris and Moore asked the Chelan Rotary Club to sponsor a contest to name the new boat. When the new boat was christened the "Speedway" she replaced the twenty-seven foot *Tenino* which had been purchased from Fred Howard to fulfill the mail contract. With the completion of the *Speedway* the boat company sold the *Tenino* to buyers in Idaho and used the money from the sale to buy a larger engine for the *Cascade Flyer*. As with the other boats the *Speedway* employed many crewmen during her years of service. Albert "Markey" Marcuson served as one of the captains of the boat for twelve years until he retired in the late 1940s. Herb Waite was also a purser and mechanic for the craft around this time. Walt Field, Earl Bryant, Bill Griffith, Henry Bell, Don Johnson, Merle Ashbaugh, and Larry Cozart were several of the *Speedway's* many pilots.

Like boats before her the *Speedway* had her share of difficulties. In September of 1931 she caught fire at the city dock when one of the engines backfired while the crew was preparing to get the boat underway. H. R. Kingman was standing on the *Speedway's* bridge when he noticed a fire in the engine compartment. Kingman yelled to Elton Dexter in the pilothouse, but before either man could do anything the fire spread rapidly to the entire cabin of the boat. Luckily there were only two passengers on board and both managed to get off the stricken craft safely. The boat company estimated that damage to the boat was about $2,000. During the repair work on the *Speedway* the owners decided to build a cabin over the main cabin. Charley Lafferty was in charge of the remodel which included installing new stage coach seats and automobile

Speedway with the pavilion in the background, above and to the right is H. W. VanSlyke's private boat the Myrju

windows. Elton Dexter assisted in the remodel and unfortunately suffered a couple of broken ribs when he fell off the boat while repainting it. The Lake Chelan Boat Company would later replace the *Speedway's* gasoline engines with two Cummins diesel engines.

During World War II the *Speedway* and Lake Chelan Boat Company crews were involved in two interesting war related events. The first occurred in late December of 1942 when boat company crew members, on their daily head of the lake run, saw a huge half-deflated barrage balloon drifting aimlessly near Stehekin. The balloon, which had broken loose from its moorings in Tacoma, was twenty-five feet in diameter, seventy-five feet long, and weighed 12,000 pounds. The balloon's mooring wires eventually got tangled in some trees high up the mountainside across from the Stehekin landing. Upper valley residents who had seen the balloon coming down hiked up and tightly secured the balloon to the trees. After boat company officials reported the balloon's whereabouts to the military the Air Force sent a detail of twenty men and an officer to retrieve the errant balloon. The *Speedway* took this group of men up lake to make their recovery in the steep terrain. The detail hiked up and carefully let out the dangerous gasses to completely deflate the balloon and then used a sled to pack it back down to load on the *Speedway*. The boat took the cargo to

Apple label featuring H. W. VanSlyke's Myrju

the Howe Sound dock in Chelan where a large crane offloaded the balloon onto a large truck. The *Mirror* interviewed one of the servicemen about the recovery and he said, "I've always wanted to be a mountain climber, but after this trip they can give this country back to the Indians." The article went on to report that these men were a special detachment whose only job was to recover lost barrage balloons.

The other incident happened almost a year later when the military lost a Lockheed Load Star two-motor airplane near the head of the lake. Apparently the plane ran out of gas and the crew all parachuted out safely after radioing their position to the home base in Tacoma. It took two weeks before searchers were able to find the craft which had gone down eleven miles above Stehekin on the north side of Junction Mountain. After the plane's discovery the military sent a salvage crew up on the Lake Chelan Boat Company's barge towed by the *Speedway*. After locating and bringing down pieces of the plane the salvagers loaded the wreckage on the barge for the trip down lake. From there the damaged plane was placed on trucks for the trip back to Tacoma.

The Boats, 1929-1998

Double-decked Speedway, around 1943, the girl in the white dress standing on the end of the dock to the left is Mary (Trainer) Bigelow

As described earlier the *Speedway* also partially sank while moored at the boat company's dock during a severe storm on January 14, 1943. In July the *Speedway* and *Cascade Flyer* were both involved in an accident when a barge the two boats were towing started to sink in the middle of the lake off of Prince Creek. The barge had thirteen horses and a load of box shooks aboard when it encountered high winds that produced large swells. The waves kept a constant barrage of water flowing over the barge which eventually loosened the caulking causing the barge to take on water. Soon the barge listed severely to one side and the box shooks slid into the lake. Fearing that the barge was going to sink the crew cut loose twelve of the horses and they started swimming ashore in opposite directions. Unfortunately, the crew could not free one of the horses and it perished when the barge sank. Another horse swam to where the lake met a steep cliff and drowned when it was unable to get out.

In December of 1948 a spectacular fire gutted the *Speedway* at the Lakeside dock. The late night fire blazed so brilliantly that it lit up the entire mountainside. After this fire the company rebuilt the boat giving it a more squared off appearance. The boat company also replaced the *Speedway's* engines, this time with two 165 horsepower GMC 6.71 Detroit Diesel engines.

Jim Courtney, a lifelong Stehekin Valley resident, remembers riding the *Speedway* when he was a young man. Jim took many winter trips on the boat when Bill Griffith, Merle Ashbaugh, and Don Johnson were pilots. Courtney recalled that on some trips passengers used rifles to shoot coyotes on the shore as the *Speedway* cruised on its run. He was quick to add that, "times have changed and you would never see that happen on today's boats." Although times may be different, Courtney stressed how important the passenger and freight vessels are for the upper valley residents. Courtney said that he takes one of the passenger boats out of Stehekin at least once a month.

During the years the *Speedway* cruised the waters of Lake Chelan the Lake Chelan Boat Company had many changes in ownership. The first change occurred in 1931 when Elton Dexter bought out Aaron Moore's share of the company. After the sale Moore and his family moved to Seattle where he operated an "auto camp" near Boeing Field. In 1942 Dave Harris sold his share of the business to George Pennell. Dexter sold his share of the boat company to Jim Lafferty and Floyd McDonald in 1946. That year the company reported that nearly 6,000 passengers had ridden the company's boats. The ownership changed again in 1948 when Walt Griffith and Richard Worden acquired the Lafferty and McDonald shares. Nine or ten years later Worden sold his interest to Paul Bryant. When Walt Griffith died in 1966 the Lake Chelan Boat Company bought out his share. In 1968 Charles Schwader purchased a small interest in the company which he gradually increased over the years. The boat company bought out George Pennell's share in 1972 following his death, leaving Paul Bryant as the majority owner of the company, with Schwader still owning a portion of the business. In 1983 both men sold out to Lake Chelan Recreation, Incorporated, jointly owned by Jack Raines, Gary Gibson, and Steve Gibson. Two years later Jack Raines acquired total ownership of the Lake Chelan Boat Company and still owns it today.

Lake Chelan Boat Company, 1998

The Boats, 1929-1998

The aging Speedway at the Lake Chelan Boat Company dock, 1998

The Lake Chelan Boat Company continued to regularly operate the *Speedway* on scheduled winter runs until they put the *Lady of the Lake II* into service in 1976. Beginning in the summer of 1983 a joint venture between the boat company and KOZI Radio used the *Speedway* to provide excursion tours. Former boat company owner, Paul Bryant, acted as the skipper and Mona Miller (Stockholm) served as hostess on these cruises. The boat made scheduled stops at Campbell's Resort, Lake Chelan Shores, Wapato Point, and the Manson dock. The cost was only five dollars and your ticket entitled you to ride the boat on any of its routes for the entire day. In an interview for the *Chelan Mirror*, KOZI's Steve Byquist said that, "visitors to the valley can have the experience of traveling on the lake for a couple of hours, instead of all day." The companies jointly operated the tour boat for two summer seasons.

As late as 1988 the company used the *Speedway* in emergencies and for special charters. Eventually the boat company permanently retired the boat and it now sits moored at their dock. In 1996 the Chelan Community Revitalization Group (CCRG), chaired by Sandra Scribner, proposed that the *Speedway* be restored and used as a museum. Jack Raines considered the boat to be a liability risk and was glad that the revitalization group wanted to take control of the boat. "We really need to get rid of it," he told the *Mirror*. Nothing happened with the CCRG's proposal because the group discovered that the *Speedway* had dry rot and would be very expensive to restore. Scribner said that parts of the old boat or a replica may be used in an expansion planned for the Chelan Chamber of Commerce Information Center. For now the old *Speedway* remains tied up at the Lake Chelan Boat Company dock. When a boat company employee, Betty Lust, accompanied the author out on the dock to photograph the boat she said that she thought Raines would give the *Speedway* to anyone who would take it. Cindy (Raines) Engstrom later said that the plan was to dismantle the *Speedway* to make dock space for their new boat. That boat is expected to arrive at the end of May, 1998.

E. B. Schley, 1937

In the spring of 1936 the Howe Sound Mining Company started construction of a tugboat and three barges. At the time the company was bringing the Holden Mine into full production and needed the tug to tow the barges, loaded with ore concentrate, from Lucerne to their dock at Chelan. A naval architect, H. C. Hansen, designed the tug to the mining company's specifications. The Winslow Marine Railway and Shipbuilding Company built the vessel and barges at Lakeside employing a crew of thirty-two men. A. W. Copp acted as the superintendent of the project for the shipbuilding company.

The shipbuilders built the tug using Douglas fir planking and Alaskan cedar for the framing and pilothouse. The builders used Australian iron bark, said to be the world's hardest wood, for the tug's sheathing and guard. They used iron for the ice skin to protect the hull from scarring when driven through the winter ice. Her deck included a pilothouse and galley; a heated forecastle had bunks for a crew of four. When completed the new tugboat was fifty-six feet long, fourteen feet nine inches wide, and had a draft of seven feet. A 160 horsepower Washington Diesel engine powered the craft by efficiently turning a fifty-six by thirty-four inch propeller. The tug had a six horsepower Regal auxiliary engine which the crew used to run an air compressor (compressed air was used to start the diesel engines).

The finished concentrate barges were eighty feet long, thirty feet wide, and had a draft of seven feet. Each barge had seven bulkheads with four watertight compartments per bulkhead. Workmen painted all the barges with cupralignum, a copper wood preservative paint, to prevent deterioration from boring insects and worms. The barges could carry up to 250 tons of ore concentrate per trip. The tug was powerful enough to tow one of the fully loaded barges the forty-two miles from Lucerne to the Howe Sound's Chelan dock in less than eight hours.

The Boats, 1929-1998

E. B. Schley and a barge at the Chelan Howe Sound dock

As the tug neared completion in the spring of 1937 there was a lot of speculation as to what the Howe Sound Mining Company would call their new vessel. The blueprints for the boat were labeled at the top with "The Chelan." The *Mirror* reported that the mining company planned to call the new boat the "Copper Queen." All the speculation about the tug's new name came to an end on Saturday, July 24 when Phyllis Post, the Lake Chelan Regatta Queen, broke a bottle of champagne over the bow and christened the new tug the *E. B. Schley*. The name was that of the head of the Howe Sound Mining Company's board of directors. The Chelan Chamber of Commerce envisioned that the launching of the new tug would be a bell-weather event to bolster the local economy and made sure it did not go unnoticed. The Chelan Junior Band, under the direction of A. W. Ruedi, performed for those assembled including city dignitaries and Howe Sound Mining Company officials. When the tug slid into the water two local men were aboard. One was the tug's new pilot, Charles Pasley, and the other was the engineer, Milo Strausbaugh. The *E. B. Schley* made its maiden voyage to Lucerne four days later pulling a barge loaded with concrete.

The first shipment of ore concentrate occurred the next spring on Saturday, April 9, 1938. The Chelan Chamber of Commerce again planned a big celebration to mark the event. The chamber encouraged private boat owners to go to Lucerne to form a flotilla to accompany the *E. B. Schley* and the barge down lake to the Howe Sound Mining dock. When the ore shipment arrived there were speeches given by chamber members, John Isenhart and Joe Stone, as well as one by George Lipsey, superintendent of the mine. Even Simon

Holden, nephew of the original holder of the Holden mine claims, was introduced to the appreciative crowd. After workmen unloaded the concentrate buckets on to trucks, a convoy of cars headed by a band proceded the trucks for a parade through Chelan.

Howe Sound Mining Company's ore concentrate buckets loaded on a truck

According to long time Chelan resident, Myrt Griffith, the trucks were a regular sight seen by Chelan residents at all hours of the day and night. With its three barges the Howe Sound Mining Company could always have one barge loading at Lucerne, another being towed by the *E. B. Schley*, while the final barge was being unloaded at Chelan. The mining company used overhead cranes at Lucerne to load the barges with containers that carried from four to five tons of ore. When a barge was fully loaded it had a total weight of 285 tons. When the ore-filled barges reached Chelan the mining company offloaded the ore onto trucks using overhead cranes. The trucks then took the concentrate to the railroad siding in Chelan Falls where cranes loaded the ore on trains bound to the smelter in Tacoma.

The Howe Sound Mining Company mainly mined copper at the Holden Mines, but gold and zinc were mined as well. During World War II the mining company started to mine zinc in greater proportions. The company claimed that they did not profit from mining zinc, but did so to support the war effort. The war also created an immense shortage of iron forcing the government to sponsor scrap iron drives to up their supplies. In 1942 alone, the *E. B. Schley* towed down barges holding 373 tons of scrap iron that the company shipped to the Bethlehem Steel plant in Seattle.

The Boats, 1929-1998

School bus accident memorial

Shortly after the war ended the *E. B. Schley* took on the grim task of helping recover the victims of a local school bus accident. The crewmen helping at the scene were Charles Pasley, Milo Strausbaugh, Floyd McDonald, and Hugh Maguire. The accident happened during an early morning snowstorm on November 26, 1945 when the bus, loaded with twenty-one passengers and the bus driver, plunged off the South Shore Road into Lake Chelan about two miles east of the State Park entrance. The bus driver, Jack Randle, and fifteen students died when the bus went down into the icy waters, plunging over 200 feet before coming to rest on a rocky shelf. An adult passenger and five students were able to escape the underwater trap by pushing through the bus windows and swimming to safety. Divers working off one of the Howe Sound Mining Company's barges found two of the bodies, but it took another five days until the divers found the bus and five more victims. The recovery team attached cables from the barge to the bus and then raised it to within twenty-five feet of the surface. Divers dove down to recover the bodies before the recovery team raised the bus another ten feet. The *E. B. Schley* then towed the barge and bus (still suspended fifteen feet below the barge) to the mining company's dock where a crane hoisted the bus onto the dock. The bodies of the nine remaining students were never found. A memorial, listing the names of the victims, now marks the spot of the accident. To this day the Lake Chelan School District does not run buses loaded with children on the South Lake Shore Road past the accident site on their regular bus routes.

Ladies of the Lake

E. B. Schley towing a loaded barge (above), picture (below) shows concentrate buckets being loaded on a barge at Lucerne

In an interview with the *Mirror* Hugh Maguire, who co-piloted the *E. B. Schley* from 1941 to 1957, said that he and Charles Pasley often used the tug and barges to help Chelan Valley residents. "We also barged supplies, cars and equipment to the mine as well as to the residents of Stehekin and Holden," Maguire commented. Earl Bryant, another longtime Lake Chelan boat pilot, got his start on the *E. B. Schley* before taking a job with the Lake Chelan Boat Company in 1955. Bryant said that the usual rotation for the tug crew was two trips on, and then one trip off. The schedule meant that crewman had to be on the lake at 3:30 a.m. to start their shifts.

The Boats, 1929-1998

The Howe Sound Mining Company continued to use the *E. B. Schley* until the Holden Mine went out of production in 1957. Eventually the company sold the tug to Joe Emerson of Scappoose, Oregon. Emerson was still using the tug as a houseboat in 1982. A recent search by the author failed to find either Emerson or the whereabouts of the old *E. B. Schley*. Tom Courtney of Stehekin at one time used an old Howe Sound barge in his shipping business, but dismantled it after he built a new barge.

Lady of the Lake, 1945

The *Lady of the Lake* was originally the *Miss Coulee*. In the late 1930s a renowned master ship builder named Shane built the hull of the *Miss Coulee* in Seattle for the Tuttle Brothers. In 1939 Gaines, Chet, and Fred "Cap" Tuttle hauled the boat to Lake Roosevelt where they finished the double decked vessel. When the Tuttles completed the boat in July of 1940 it was sixty-five feet long, seventeen feet wide, and drew four feet of water. Two 200 horsepower Cummins Diesel engines powered the fifty-four ton craft. The Tuttles used the *Miss Coulee* as a tour boat behind Grand Coulee dam. They ran daylong excursions that left Spokane at 9:00 a.m. and arrived in Coulee Dam at 1:45 p.m. The fare from Miles, which was just north of Davenport, to Coulee Dam was $4.00. Chet Tuttle piloted the *Miss Coulee* on her sight-seeing tours and excursion trips. Her upper deck had a refreshment and soft drink bar and the lower deck was used for dancing. Chet remarked that he had "been operating boats for over 30 years now and never had I found one that handles as pretty or runs as nicely as *Miss Coulee*." Unfortunately, an international crisis would soon force the Tuttles to give up their cherished craft.

Miss Coulee

Ladies of the Lake

The start of World War II caused a drastic drop in tourism, so in 1942 the Tuttles sold the *Miss Coulee* to the Grand Coulee Navigation Company. The navigation company used the boat to tow logs, but late in 1944 sold the wooden boat to the Lake Chelan Boat Company for $25,000. In 1945 the boat company paid Beardmore Transfer $1,555 to haul the *Miss Coulee*, with her upper cabin removed, to Lake Chelan. Each time the movers reached a viaduct they had to unload the boat and put it on rollers to get it through the underpass. When the movers reached the old trestle bridge at Brewster they had to unload the boat again and pull the boat across on rollers. As the hauler's truck pulled the boat across, there was only a four inch clearance on either side. The hauling crew then reloaded the *Miss Coulee* on the truck for the remaining trip to Chelan. There the boat company launched the boat and reinstalled her top cabin.

The Lake Chelan Boat Company remodeled their newly acquired boat by repainting it white with a green trim. Inside, the company added modern deck chairs to compliment her mahogany accents. The refurbished boat could easily accommodate 150 passengers. In the spring of 1945 the boat company held a "name the boat" contest cosponsored by the Rotary Club, Lions Club, and the Chamber of Commerce. The contest received over 2,000 entries of which 111 contestants had submitted: *Lady of the Lake*. On April 9, the day of the christening, Vern Beckman presented Mrs. Martin Schendel of Chelan Falls a fifty dollar War Bond for her *Lady of the Lake* entry. Phil Clampitt and W. H. Worden had assisted Beckman with the judging of the entries.

Lady of the Lake

The Boats, 1929-1998

Later that day a crowd of 300 people gathered at the city dock to attend the christening ceremony for the newly named *Lady of the Lake*. As the boat neared the dock after its trip from Lakeside the Chelan High School band played the "Star Spangled Banner." Charles Lund acted as master of ceremonies for the program and M. E. Field gave a brief sketch of the history of boat navigation on Lake Chelan. The highlight of the program came when Patty Pennell, Mr. and Mrs. George Pennell's fourteen year old daughter, christened the *Lady*. Patty broke a bottle of burgundy on the bow while in a rowboat manned by two Sea Scouts, Bernard Trainer and Ronald Kercheval. Then as the crew started the *Lady's* engines the high school band played "Anchors Aweigh." The boat company provided free passes to all in attendance and encouraged everyone to board the boat for a cruise to Twenty Five Mile Creek and back. The *Lady* spent most of the afternoon making trips up and down the lake. Teachers from the Chelan schools brought their pupils for rides and for many students it was their first boat ride on Lake Chelan.

In 1946 the Lake Chelan Boat Company completely refurbished the *Lady of the Lake*. The Howe Sound Mining Company allowed the boat company the use of their shop and machinery to do the remodeling. Ted Fulton did much of the interior carpentry work which included making new cabinets (they also served as seats) to stow life preservers on the upper deck, installing a mahogany railing on the back deck, and creating a small mahogany refreshment bar on the lower deck. When the boat company completed the work in July of that year they emphasized that the boat's two 250 horsepower Hall Scott engines had been enclosed in insulated cases to prevent engine noise from reaching the passengers. Boat company officials told the *Mirror* that it had been a "gigantic task" to renovate the *Lady*. They were especially excited to reveal that a new public address system had been installed with a microphone in the pilothouse that would allow the crew to point out items of interest to the passengers.

That fall the *Lady of the Lake* hosted seventy educators who were members of the North Central Washington Athletics Association and the Schoolmasters Association. The athletic association conducted their meeting while the boat made its way up lake. When the *Lady* arrived in Stehekin both groups disembarked to have dinner at the Golden West Lodge. Educators representing the Lake Chelan School District were Morgen Owings (superintendent), Lowell Poore, Ray Votapka, Richard Louis, Robert Coppola, and Robert Loidhamer.

After the remodel the Lake Chelan Boat Company continued using the *Lady of the Lake* as its regular passenger boat to Stehekin. The boat faithfully made the run to the head of the lake until the bitterly cold winter weather of 1948-49 completely froze the lake from Chelan to a point near the Yacht Club.

Ladies of the Lake

Old Chelan Box and Manufacturing pilings in Mill Bay

The U. S. Forest Service had at first tried to keep a channel broken using their steel landing barge, but for a two week period the lake froze solid from six to ten inches thick. During that time the boat company and the Howe Sound Mining tug and barges shipped all their freight and ore from Twenty Five Mile Creek. George Pennell reported that at the Lake Chelan Boat Company dock the lake temperature was thirty-seven degrees down to twenty feet. Eventually a strong wind blowing off the face of Stormy Mountain and down the First Creek drainage started to break up the ice. When the ice broke and started to move at the Chelan Box and Manufacturing Company, at what is now called Mill Bay, it sheared off the mill's pilings at the water line. The next winter was also harsh as the lake again froze over above Manson, and the lake temperature dipped to thirty-three degrees.

In February of 1949 the *Lady of the Lake* hosted a "Camera Cruise." Green's Drug sponsored the event, which was reminiscent of the once popular winter excursions on the old *Cascade Flyer*. George Dissmore, who was in charge of Green's camera department, planned the event. During the cruise, pilots George Pennell and Walt Field stopped or slowed the boat anytime there was something interesting to see or photograph. The passengers saw many mountain goats and were able to photograph a deer swimming the lake near Lucerne. On their return many of the cruise participants said it was the best trip they had ever taken up lake. The following year seventy people took the camera cruise and were similarly impressed with the beauty and magnificence that Lake Chelan offered in the winter.

The Boats, 1929-1998

In the spring of 1951 the Lake Chelan Boat Company took the *Lady of the Lake* out of service for an overhaul. The *Chelan Valley Mirror* reported that the *Lady* had "been completely redecorated, refinished, thoroughly cleaned and painted and in general fixed up until now she is the smoothest and quietest boat on the lake." The boat company completed the repair work by early summer and then put her back in service. Of the *Lady of the Lake's* first run to Stehekin since her refurbishing the *Mirror* commented, "over 100 passengers were aboard and all had plenty of room and freedom of movement all over both decks of the boat." The *Lady* would continue as the boat company's flagship for another twenty-five years.

Lady of the Lake and the Speedway at the Stehekin landing, 1962

In an article written for the *National Geographic Magazine* in the early 1960s writer Edwards Park chronicled not only the beauty of Lake Chelan, but the lives of the people living and working in the North Cascades. In his acccount he wrote of the *Lady of the Lake's* impact on people's lives. Park gave this example of one of the *Lady's* many daily interactions:

> **Bucking a headwind, the vessel plowed steadily through choppy water as flanking hills grew to mighty crags. We eased toward shore at Canoe Creek, aiming for a tiny dock where an elderly, straight-backed woman waited for us. Behind her, in a sunny clearing, stood a log cabin.**

Ladies of the Lake

>As we nosed in to the dock, our mate leaned from the gunwale with a couple of letters. She took them and waved, and we veered away.
>
>"Mrs. [Ida] Pilz lives there all alone," the skipper told me. "Used to shoot bears when they raided her berry patch, but they got too heavy for her to move away. Now she shoos them off with a broom. Quite a girl. We're about the only people she sees."

The *Lady of the Lake* was a welcome intrusion to the serenity and peacefulness to be found up lake. People there depended on the *Lady* and the other boats to provide a connection to the outside world.

When the Chelan Boat Company launched the *Lady of the Lake II* in 1976 they took the little *Lady* off the regular run, and from then on used her on the winter run and for charters. On the night of August 30, 1984 the *Lady of the Lake* sank at the Chelan Boat Company dock, because a hatch was inadvertently left open. The sinking extensively damaged the boat's engines and interior requiring a complete refurbishing. Crews installed two 6.71 Detroit Diesels that would give the boat a cruising speed of fifteen miles per hour. On the inside they added more insulation to make the *Lady* more comfortable on her winter runs and tables were installed so she could be used as a dinner charter boat in the summer. After the boat company completed the work in the spring of 1985, the little *Lady* returned to serve as the regular passenger boat until the *Lady II* took over for the summer season which began on May 15.

The *Lady of the Lake* has had many pilots and crew members over the years. Claude W. Southwick, Bill Foote, Charles Foote, Ernie Pershall, Frank Huni, Claude R. Southwick, Earl Bryant, Bill Griffith, and Ken Wilsey have all piloted the boat.

Lake Chelan Boat Company charter coordinator, Nancy Clapp, said that the *Lady of the Lake* has hosted countless charters. Her personal favorite was a charter for only two people and lasted just one hour. Nancy explained that a young man wanted to propose to his girlfriend on the *Lady*. The day of the special charter the man convinced his future fiancée that they were just going on a regular passenger trip, but she was skeptical because they were the only passengers. After the boat left the dock the young man took his puzzled girlfriend to a table adorned with a fancy tablecloth and flowers on the back deck of the boat. There the man proposed to his startled girlfriend. It is assumed that the couple sailed off into the sunset and lived happily ever after.

In 1990 the Lake Chelan Boat Company took the *Lady of the Lake* off the winter Stehekin run after they put the *Lady Express* into service. As of 1998

The Boats, 1929-1998

Lady of the Lake at the Lake Chelan Boat Company dock, 1998

the boat company still used the *Lady of the Lake* as a general work boat and for charters, but she has not served as a passenger boat since the company put the *Lady Express* into service in 1990. The boat company plans to retire the little *Lady* when they launch their newest boat in May of 1998. At that time the Chelan Community Revitalization Group may take control of the boat. The community group did not have any definite plans, but one suggestion was to use the little *Lady* as a floating restaurant.

Allen Stone, 1946

In March of 1946 George Pennell of the Lake Chelan Boat Company bought an Army surplus twenty-one pontoon barge in Lathrop, California for $1,700. The barge replaced an old wooden barge that the company had previously used. To push the barge Pennell purchased a Sea Mule, pilothouse, and a power unit for an additional $1,200. George Pennell named the barge the *Allen Stone*, after a man who was a local jack of all trades. Over the years Stone had built several highly crafted boats for use on the lake. His best known boat was the *Radio*. According to a former boat company owner, Charles Schwader, after the company built the freight barge it was unnamed. Stone, who then lived at Twin Harbor, asked Pennell when he was going to get around to naming a boat after him. Pennell was ready to put the barge into service, so he named it the *Allen Stone*.

Ladies of the Lake

Allen Stone being used to place a buoy in front of Dick and Ginny Tessier's Wapato Point home, 1997

In August of 1951 the *Allen Stone* helped in the recovery of a plane and its pilot from Lake Chelan. The plane, piloted by Earl Schmitten of Cashmere, had clipped the Washington Water Power cables that once crossed the lake above Manson. It then crashed and sank near Watson's Harverene Resort. The accident occurred about 6:00 p.m. on a Saturday and by the next day divers from Grand Coulee Dam were trying to recover the plane and its pilot. Diving from the deck of the *Allen Stone*, the divers could not locate any wreckage and suspended the search. The next day a Seattle diver, David McCray, and seventeen employees from Schmitten's sawmill in Cashmere resumed the search. Along with law enforcement officers and crew members from the *Allen Stone* the wreckage was found and hauled to the surface. It appeared that Schmitten had survived the crash, but then drowned when the plane submerged in the lake.

In 1956 the boat company acquired another nine pontoons for $1,100 which increased the *Allen Stone's* deck space to twenty-one by sixty-five feet. Her overall length, including the pilothouse, was eighty-one feet. In 1968 the company replaced the vessel's original 90 horsepower Hudson Invader engine with a 165 horsepower Detroit Diesel engine. In 1990 the boat company added twenty more pontoons giving the *Allen Stone* a deck space of thirty-five by eighty feet. The barge cruises at a leisurely seven miles per hour and takes two days to make a round-trip to the head of the lake.

The Boats, 1929-1998

The *Allen Stone* can carry up to 100 tons of freight. Over the years the barge has carried a varied cargo including hay, food, gravel, building supplies, furniture, household appliances, livestock, automobiles, well-drilling rigs, and even a sixty ton rock crusher. The barge has carried as many as forty horses for the Courtney family in Stehekin and shipped kid goats from there for a man who raised them commercially. The barge also pushes a pile driver used to install docks.

On a typical run to Stehekin the *Allen Stone* averages about five stops per trip, but it is not unusual for the barge to make ten to twelve stops. She always lands at Lucerne so that supplies for Holden Village can be offloaded. The barge typically leaves Chelan at 4:30 or 5:00 a.m. and it takes about nine hours to make the trip to the head of the lake. The crew works four-hour shifts on the regular trips. When they are not on duty they nap or read in living quarters found in the lower part of the pilothouse. Over the years crew members have included: Ben Little, Mickey McMorrow, Bill Flick, Willis Griffith, Earl Bryant, Larry Cozart, Charles Schwader, Vernon (Pat) Risley, Henry Bell, Corwyn Fischer, Sam Bryant, Chris Raines, "Brick" Harris, Larry Majchrzak, and Bill Sachse.

Usually there is little excitement involved in the operation of the *Allen Stone*. The biggest concern is that the barge is carefully loaded so that her load is evenly balanced. The weight at the rear is kept the heaviest so that the propeller stays deep in the water. In 1975 the *Allen Stone* overturned at the Lake Chelan Boat Company dock as the crew was loading it. When the mishap occurred it sent a crane, a container of gasoline, and two dump trucks loaded with gravel to the bottom of the lake. The accident left the barge floating upside down until the boat company's crane righted it.

The *Allen Stone* continues to operate on Lake Chelan today. The highlight for many Chelan Valley residents is when the barge comes to Manson Bay for the annual Fourth of July fireworks show. The *Allen Stone* is always the last to arrive for the celebration that brings out hundreds of boats and people from all around. The barge's deck is jam packed with fireworks as she silently and inconspicuously enters the bay for the late evening display. After the festivities the *Allen Stone* returns to Chelan among the throngs of horn tooting boats. Many newcomers to this Independence Day activity never even realize that the 100 ton barge is there. Jack Raines has provided the *Allen Stone* for the fireworks display as a community service ever since he acquired the Lake Chelan Boat Company in 1983.

Ladies of the Lake

Lady of the Lake II, 1976

The *Lady of the Lake II* was built because of one man's dream and another man's determination. In 1961 after George Pennell, a Lake Chelan Boat Company co-owner, conceived the idea to build a steel-hulled boat he asked one of his newer employees if he would build it for him. That employee, Larry Cozart, was a former California cotton farmer who had originally come to Chelan on vacation the year before. Cozart was not a stranger to the area as he had gown up on his father's Entiat orchard and his wife, Bertha, was a Manson native. Then in his early fifties, Cozart decided he was not ready to retire so he took a job with the boat company working two days a week as a deckhand on the *Allen Stone*. After three months Cozart took over as barge master when Pennell promoted Willis Griffith to be the pilot of the little *Lady of the Lake*. Soon the company discovered Cozart's excellent welding skills and had him doing general boat maintenance and repair as well. Pennell had been especially impressed with Cozart's steel work rebuilding the cab of the *Allen Stone*. It did not take Pennell long to realize that Cozart was the man he needed to build his new boat.

When Pennell first raised the possibility of constructing a new boat with Cozart, the welder told his boss that he thought he and Bill Flick, another boat company employee, could do the job. Pennell asked Cozart to keep the project secret because he feared that Chelan Valley residents would not accept a steel-hulled boat. Every previous passenger boat on the lake had been made of wood and Pennell knew he was competing with over eighty years of boat building tradition. Pennell planned to have Cozart build his new craft in stages as the boat company had extra money to put into the endeavor. The undertaking was definitely a "pay-as-you-go" proposition for the company. In 1968 Pennell incurred the first expense by hiring Edwin Monk, a Seattle boat designer, to draw up the plans for the hull of the 100 foot vessel. When Cozart saw the plans he asked Monk to redesign the bow to a clipper type because he knew the original plan would not work on Lake Chelan. Cozart wanted a new boat that would be able to nose its way into shallow landings to pick up or leave off passengers. The boat's design from the hull up, except for some detail around the pilothouse, would be almost entirely Cozart's.

When there was more money to actually start the project Cozart started to work with the help of Charles Schwader because Bill Flick had by then been killed in a plane accident. Cozart taught Schwader what he knew about welding, and Schwader was an asset because of his drafting and blueprint reading experience. Together the pair made a solid shipbuilding team. After studying up on shipbuilding procedures Cozart and Schwader first laid out the keel's full-size plan on a 100 foot driveway adjacent to a Blue Chelan warehouse.

The Boats, 1929-1998

*Lady of the Lake II at the Lake Chelan Boat Company dock, 1998
(note the aging Speedway in background, right)*

Soon Pennell had a workshop built with a floor large enough to put down a twenty-four by eighteen foot grid, sectioned in one foot squares. Cozart and Schwader used the grid to identify problems with the boat's design. Once they had done this they laid out the boat full scale using plywood sheets to make a pattern for the boat. By 1969, with help from Paul Bryant and others, the steel frame of the boat took shape. Within two years Cozart had stockpiled fifteen frames and five bulkheads, enough material to frame a boat 100 feet long and twenty-four feet wide, on the Goodfellow Fill just to the south of the boat company's dock.

By December of 1971 Cozart and his team had completed all of the framing for the boat using steel bridge girders. The crew constructed a working 120 by thirty foot base made of steel bridge girders that was partly over water and partly over land. The base provided a level baseline for the keel. Then the shipbuilders laid the keel of the vessel using an A-frame trolley hoist that Cozart had designed and built. Using the hoist the crew could lift and place the two ton steel girders into their precise position.

While work on the boat progressed George Pennell was fighting a personal battle with cancer. Pennell had been spending less time at the boat company, but one day in 1972 his wife, Ruth, drove him down to check on the construction of the boat. He seemed very pleased with the work done so far, but

Ladies of the Lake

his real concern may have been to get assurances from Cozart that the boat would be completed. In a *Mirror* article, Cozart told reporter Gaylen Willett that he "promised [Pennell] that I would see it through to completion." Cozart thought that this was the last time his boss saw the boat. George Pennell died later that year in June.

After Pennell's death Charles Schwader took over more management of the Lake Chelan Boat Company and was not able to help Cozart as much. John Gordon, another welder, joined Cozart and by 1973 they had completed plating the hull and framing the cabin. By the fall of the next year the shipbuilders had finished the installation of the rudders and the propellers and their shafts. After thirteen long years Cozart was finally ready to launch the hull of Pennell's dream boat.

In October of 1974 the Lake Chelan Boat Company launched the eighty ton hull. Patty Risley, George Pennell's daughter, tearfully christened the shell the *Lady of the Lake II* with a bottle of champagne as she rode the hull into the water. Patty had also christened the boat company's first *Lady of the Lake* almost thirty years earlier. Steve Byquist of KOZI Radio remembered that there was a tremendous screeching sound as bulldozers helped push the hull into the water. Cozart would later describe the launching as "a screaming, squallering trip." Patty Risley said that the first thing Cozart did when the boat entered the water was to go down and inspect the hull. Soon he reappeared on deck with a big smile and exclaimed, "She's watertight!" Risley said that Cozart was extremely proud of his crew's workmanship.

The work on the new *Lady* was far from finished. Over the next fourteen months Cozart and his crew literally had tons of work to do. During that time span they used a crane to install two 12.71 Detroit Diesel engines, two 500 gallon diesel fuel tanks, and holding tanks for sanitation. The boat builders also decked the upper cabin and rear observation deck, and roofed the upper cabin and pilothouse. Charles Schwader even made the steering wheel for the boat which incorporated a center bolt salvaged from the lake by Paul Bryant. In December of 1975 the boat was still without seats or windows, but the builders took the vessel out on its first shakedown cruise. Other than some minor mechanical adjustments the ship performed very well. The *Lady*, pushed by two propellers about three and one-half feet in diameter, easily reached the boat's cruising speed of eighteen miles per hour.

Work continued on the *Lady of the Lake II* into the winter. While installing windows designed and made in Wenatchee, one of the big windows fell overboard and came to rest at the bottom of the lake. Although still uncompleted, the *Lady* unofficially took her maiden voyage to Stehekin on Christmas Eve of 1975 when the passenger boat, *Speedway*, unexpectedly filled

The Boats, 1929-1998

Lady of the Lake II cruising up lake past Wapato Point

with holiday travelers. The Lake Chelan Boat Company seized on the opportunity to test their new boat. Claude Southwick said that the boat company also realized a large tax write-off by using the boat before the end of the year. It was not the most comfortable ride for the sixteen passengers making the trip. The seats had not arrived from the manufacturer in Michigan so the passengers had to use folding chairs. Workmen had not installed either the carpet nor the insulation so it was a cold and noisy ride, but it did get the travelers to their destination. The trip also gave Chelan Valley residents their first glimpse of the sleek new ship that would soon be making regular runs later in the year. After that first up lake run Paul Bryant jokingly told the *Mirror*, "What really happened was that the reindeer got sick that day and we had to get Santa Claus in." When the *Lady* returned to Chelan Cozart and his crew spent the next several months installing the insulation, carpet, seats, and a multitude of other items. When completed the new boat weighed in the neighborhood of 100 tons, and had a six foot draft.

In June of 1976 the Lake Chelan Boat Company requested an operating license from the Marine Division of the Department of Labor and Industries. The department licensed the boat for 350 passengers. A letter from an insurance company surveyor who had inspected the boat especially pleased Cozart. A portion of the letter read, "The workmanship on this vessel is far better than I have seen in many of the larger yards in the area." To get the boat in such tiptop shape had cost the boat company more than $188,000. Cozart, who was sixty-six years old when the *Lady* was finally completed, then quit his job. He later said that he "left the boat company at this time, feeling all my promises and obligations had been fulfilled." The "retired" cotton farmer would now really retire. It had been fifteen years since he signed on with the boat company to work a couple of days a week as a deckhand.

That summer the *Lady of the Lake II* performed her job admirably, but was never filled to capacity. Her pilots for the first season included Claude R. Southwick, Gary Cooper and Earl Bryant, plus the boat company's owners Charles Schwader and Paul Bryant. Also piloting vessels for the boat company during this time were Butch Billington, Jim Russell, Jeff Clapstein, Gardner Hart, and Henry Bell. By the season's end there had been some mishaps and problems, but nothing not to be expected when shaking down a new 100 foot ship. The boat company planned various projects in the off-season for the *Lady*. These included adding steps off the prow for loading passengers more easily, building new cargo space under the front deck, adjusting doors throughout the boat, and giving the outside of the boat another coat of paint.

The Lake Chelan Boat Company's flagship *Lady of the Lake II* quickly established herself as the most dependable passenger boat on the lake. Because of her steel construction, fires and sinkings quickly became a memory of a bygone era. Every year thousands of Chelan Valley residents and tourists ride the *Lady* or benefit from the freight and mail that she carries. Upper valley residents even use the boat as their grocery delivery service. When these residents want a load of grocery items they send a list and a signed blank check to a Chelan grocery store. At Safeway employees use the list to shop for the goods, and after they are checked out the groceries are put in the storeroom. In the summer the boat company sends someone over every day to pick up the boxed grocery orders for shipping up lake. Safeway does not charge for this service and the boat company collects only a nominal shipping fee. Alice Adams, a Safeway employee, said that in the summer the store receives about five or six requests a week for groceries, and that orders also increase during holiday periods.

If you have ridden on the *Lady of the Lake II* in recent years you may have noticed a photo gallery by the snack bar advertising weddings aboard the boat. The couple in the photographs is Mark and Barb Marney of Chelan. They were married on board the *Lady* on July 28, 1984. The 150 guests boarded the boat that day with the anxious bride and groom around 8:00 p.m. and began cruising up lake. Just as the sun began to dip behind the mountains the captain, Corwyn Fischer, stopped the boat and the ceremony began. Framed by the spectacular scenery and a red hued sky, the couple said, "I do." The boat then continued the cruise and the guests were treated to a night of lively dancing and celebration. Almost fourteen years and two children later, the Marneys have wonderful memories of their wedding on the *Lady*. "We did have a captive audience, but they all seemed to be having a great time," Barb said.

The Boats, 1929-1998

Barb and Mark Marney, married aboard the Lady of the Lake II, July 28, 1984

Ladies of the Lake

Lady of the Lake II at the Stehekin landing, 1997

In 1986 Julie Southwick became a pilot on the *Lady of the Lake II* and a third-generation Southwick Lake Chelan passenger boat skipper. Julie's grandfather, Claude W. Southwick, had captained the *Comet, Comanche, Liberty,* and *Cascade Flyer.* Her father, Claude R. Southwick, was a longtime pilot of both the *Lady I* and the *Lady II.* A September 1987 article about Julie, written by *Wenatchee World* reporter, Hu Blonk, was headlined "This lady of the lake is the skipper." Blonk wrote that Julie had started working aboard the *Lady II* four years earlier at the snack bar, and then progressed to deckhand where she "got a taste of the wheel." Southwick eventually moved up to purser, before finally taking on her duties as skipper. She then shared a work schedule of four days on, three days off with two other pilots — Chris Raines and Ken Wilsey. After several years of piloting the *Lady II* Julie Southwick left Chelan and spent some time working on the National Oceanic and Atmospheric Administration (NOAA) research ship, *Discoverer.* When Julie was a crew member on that vessel it cruised the Central Pacific studying El Niño. Southwick now works in Seattle installing fiber optic security systems. Those who knew Julie said that she was a competent and feisty *Lady II* pilot.

Besides the *Lady of the Lake II's* regular runs the boat company also uses her for countless charters. In the spring, around graduation time, the festively decorated boat is out on the lake almost every evening with partying high school seniors. Many school groups use the boat for field trips to Holden Village and to the head of the lake. Often conventioneers entertain on the *Lady II* in conjunction with their business meetings. In the past there have been many different types of comedy, dancing, and dinner cruises. Every Christmas season

The Boats, 1929-1998

Lady of the Lake, Lady of the Lake II, Speedway, and Allen Stone at Lake Chelan Boat Company dock, 1998

the Lake Chelan Boat Company donates the use of the boat for a caroling cruise. The boat crew collects a minimum of two dollars from every passenger and the money is donated to a local food bank. The *Lady II* seems to be able to accommodate every occasion and celebration.

Lady Express, 1990

In February of 1990 Jack Raines, owner of the Lake Chelan Boat Company, announced that construction was underway on a new boat. Munson Marine of Edmonds, Washington was building the all-aluminum vessel which would be sixty-five feet long and twenty-one feet wide. Raines said that planning for the boat had been ongoing for over two years. The specifications called for a V-shaped planing hull designed to produce a quickly dissipating low wake. The craft, already named the *Lady Express*, was to travel at a cruising speed of thirty miles per hour which meant that a trip to the head of the lake would take only two hours. The tentative summer schedule called for the *Lady Express* to stop only at Field's Point on the up lake trip to Stehekin, and at Lucerne and Field's Point on the return run. In the winter the *Lady Express* would replace the *Lady of the Lake II* as the only boat making regular passenger and freight runs up lake.

Ladies of the Lake

Little Lady of the Lake assisting with the launch of the Lady Express (note that the Lady Express does not have her top cabin installed)

The boat company planned to operate the boat with a 100 passenger capacity even though the boat had the ability to carry more people. If the boat company adopted the new schedule, passengers taking the new express boat could leave Chelan at 8:30 a.m. and arrive in Stehekin at 10:30 a.m. After a one hour layover, the boat would start on its return at 11:30 and arrive back in Chelan at 1:30 p.m. (the present day schedule is not the same). If travelers arranged to take a return trip on the *Lady II* they would be able to have a three hour layover at the head of the lake. Raines told the *Mirror* that the new boat would give tourists more options, and if they took a round-trip on the *Lady Express* it would give them most of the afternoon to spend in Chelan.

With the start of construction of the *Lady Express* on February 1, Munson Marine ran two crews to keep the project on schedule. Near the end of February, the boat builders had tacked the vessel's hull in place and were busy installing her four bulkheads. The builders would place an additional front collision bulkhead as the work progressed. It was twelve feet from the boat's keel to the top of the hull and one could already see the sleek appearance of the new boat emerging. Munson Marine had promised to finish the *Lady Express*, except for attaching the upper cabin and railings, by June 22, 1990. The final assembly of the boat would take place in Chelan.

Munson Marine finished the *Lady Express* well ahead of schedule and was ready to ship the boat to Lake Chelan on Tuesday, June 12, 1990. Associated Boat Transport, Inc., of Seattle undertook the huge job of moving the thirty-

The Boats, 1929-1998

Jack Raines, Lake Chelan Boat Company owner, tossing a line to tie up his new boat

plus ton boat. A truck towed a lowboy trailer carrying the hull with its lower cabin in place. Transport driver, Mark Wolfe, left Edmonds that Tuesday about 1:00 a.m. towing the trailer and traveled over Snoqualmie Pass, arriving in Cle Elum, Washington around 9:00 a.m. The boat movers left Cle Elum the next morning at 6:00 a.m. continuing on towards Lake Chelan. They took a route up Narvarre Coulee, so that they could bypass the Knapps Tunnel on Highway 97A, and then continued down the South Shore Road toward Chelan.

The *Lady Express* arrived at the Lake Chelan Boat Company around 10:15 a.m. on June 13. After some tricky maneuvering of the lowboy trailer and a timely push by a front-end loader, the crew finally launched the new boat at 11:17 a.m. There was no ceremony accompanying the launching, but about fifty spectators cheered when the boat entered the water. Claude Southwick, piloting the little *Lady of the Lake*, came alongside the rudderless *Lady Express* and crew members secured a line to tow the new craft to the boat company dock.

During the next week construction crews joined the top cabin and railings to the top of the *Lady Express's* lower cabin. On June 20 the Lake Chelan Boat Company was ready to put their new craft through some high speed runs to check her performance on the water. Bill Munson of Munson

Ladies of the Lake

Marine was aboard to help evaluate the seaworthiness of the new boat. Although small problems showed up during these tests the *Lady Express* proved to be a stable and speedy craft. Her twin double turbocharged and after cooled V-12x92 Detroit Diesel engines sped the vessel along at an estimated speed of thirty-five miles per hour at 2400 RPM. Jack Raines later told the *Mirror* that the boat would be operated at an optimum of 1900 RPM (approximately twenty-eight miles per hour) to conserve fuel once the boat was on its regular passenger runs.

Munson told the *Mirror* that there were many tests that the *Lady Express* had to pass before the Coast Guard would certify the new boat. One of these tests was to evaluate whether the new boat's noise level met acceptable limits. To ensure that the boat operated within these standards the builders installed two huge glasspack mufflers. Another test the *Lady Express* had to pass was a wake analysis to make sure that her wake would not damage the shoreline. To do this study Munson Marine used a U. S. Navy software program and entered wake configuration data from the *Lady of the Lake II*. The program compared wake statistics from the *Lady II* to evaluate how the *Lady Express's* wake would impact Lake Chelan's shoreline. The study determined that the new boat had a wake that was one foot less tall, much flatter, and dissipated quicker than that of the *Lady II*.

After Munson Marine and the Lake Chelan Boat Company completed all the testing and final adjustments the *Lady Express* made her maiden voyage to Stehekin on July 14, 1990. She left the boat company dock shortly after the *Lady of the Lake II* departed at 8:30 a.m. and quickly overtook the larger vessel. Jack Raines and Claude Southwick shared the piloting duties on the inaugural trip. Other crewmen aboard were maintenance man, Larry Majchrzak, and snack bar operator, Tim Hanes. Among the passengers were two special guests — Charles Schwader, a former part-owner of the boat company, and Earl Bryant, a twenty year veteran boat pilot. About sixty-five regular passengers, most making round-trips, boarded the *Lady Express* at Chelan with several more getting on at Field's Point. One couple were newlyweds from New Hampshire en route to their honeymoon at the head of the lake. On the return trip another twenty-five people came aboard at Lucerne to bring the passenger count to nearly ninety travelers.

Two sheriff's boats escorted the *Lady Express* to just past Field's Point and one stayed with the express boat from there back to Chelan. Although there were a few minor problems and concerns about the pitch of the props the boat performed as expected. The *Lady Express* arrived in Stehekin at 10:55 a.m. and returned to Chelan by 2:55 p.m. The new boat made quite an impression on most of the passengers. Tom Yunghans of Fullerton, California told the *Mirror*

The Boats, 1929-1998

reporter, Jon Nuxoll, that he "would like to waterski" behind the *Lady Express*. Boat company owner, Jack Raines, had previously pledged to ski behind the sleek new craft, "whenever time will allow me." So far Raines has not kept his promise, but from time to time his employees remind him of his vow.

On a crisp and sunny day in February, 1998 the author enjoyed the unique experience of riding the *Lady Express* on a round-trip to the head of Lake Chelan. Passengers boarding the boat at the Lake Chelan Boat Company dock were welcomed by the crew consisting of Ken Wilsey, Nancy Clapp, and Shawn Raines. Although all three were pilots, Ken Wilsey, a twenty year senior pilot, skippered the boat that day. Raines acted as purser, while Clapp served as deckhand and snack bar hostess. It was obvious to the passengers that the crew enjoyed their jobs and the camaraderie associated with working as a team was very evident.

Senior Pilot, Ken Wilsey, scanning the water ahead of the Lady Express

About twenty-five passengers were aboard when the *Lady Express* left the dock promptly at 10:00 a.m., and another eight to ten got on at Field's Point. The passengers ran the gamut of daily sightseers to up lake locals. Typical of the first category were Bob and Julie Star of Vancouver, Washington who were making the day trip with their son, Rob, and Julie's mother, Lucille

Ladies of the Lake

Eubanks. They had been staying at Wapato Point on a timeshare exchange, and having never been to Lake Chelan decided to take the daylong cruise. One of the many locals riding the *Lady Express* that day was Jim Courtney, a descendent of a pioneering Stehekin family, accompanied by his wife and small children. For the Courtneys the boat ride was a regular experience, although Jim wished they did not have to come down lake as much. But with business to attend to, the children's doctor's visits, and various other family needs the trips were inconvenient, but necessary. Their life is not unlike many permanent up lake residents. When the Courtney's children complete eighth grade at the small Stehekin School they will have to be homeschooled or sent to live in places like Chelan or Wenatchee to finish their education. Whatever the sacrifices, one senses that Jim Courtney would not have it any other way.

As the *Lady Express* cruised effortlessly atop the water toward Stehekin, Nancy Clapp attended to every passenger's need or question. Nancy is only the second woman to pilot a passenger boat on Lake Chelan. Usually she pilots the *Lady Express* during the summer season, but on this trip she graciously operated the small snack bar found in the back of the lower cabin. Besides dispensing drinks and snacks Nancy effortlessly fielded questions from intrigued tourists and this inquisitive writer. When the boat made its stops Nancy was out on the back of the boat welcoming passengers and flinging freight. She is the type of employee every company needs — hard working and personable.

Senior pilot, Ken Wilsey, was at the wheel as the *Lady Express* wound its way to the head of the lake. Wilsey, who has the most seniority of any active pilot, operated the vessel with a quiet calm. Even when purser, Shawn Raines, verbally jabbed at the purposeful Wilsey he rarely, if ever, let his eyes avert from scanning the water ahead of the swiftly moving craft. Wilsey's slight smile gave a hint that Raines' playful comments would not go unchallenged when the two were together without the prying eyes of an intruder. When the boat finally reached Stehekin at about 12:30 p.m., Wilsey and the rest of the crew secured the boat for the ninety minute stopover. After eating lunch Nancy Clapp went to visit with friends at the landing store, while Wilsey and Raines hunkered down for a few games of cribbage.

A loud blast of the *Lady Express's* air horn signaled to passengers that it was time to begin boarding for the trip to Chelan. Within minutes tourists, many of whom had recently returned from a bus tour to Rainbow Falls, meandered aboard the waiting craft. Soon Shawn Raines, who had taken over piloting duties from Ken Wilsey, gently backed the *Lady Express* out of its berth and evenly accelerated until it reached a smooth plane. When the boat neared Lucerne Raines looked to see if anyone was there to flag the boat for a stop. With no one on the dock Raines veered the boat slightly to the left and continued down and across the lake toward Canoe Creek to deliver some mail.

The Boats, 1929-1998

Nancy Clapp, Lady Express crew member and summer season pilot

Ladies of the Lake

Lady Express, Stehekin landing

The Boats, 1929-1998

Field's Point landing

Once at the creek the *Lady Express* slowed as it approached the shoreline and Raines and Wilsey looked for any sign of activity. After a few moments Nancy Yount emerged from a lakeside home and ran to the end of a dock. With the lake level down the *Lady Express* could not reach the dock so Raines yelled at Nancy to go to a place further up the shore where he thought he could nudge the boat in close enough to deliver the single letter. As the boat inched forward Wilsey spread-eagled himself off the front of the bow to hand the letter to the eager woman. The passengers cheered after Wilsey had successfully delivered the mail. However, the event gave new meaning to the old mail slogan, "Through sleet and snow..." The axiom should be revised to include "low water" as well.

The *Lady Express* continued on its way down lake and finally reached Field's Point where several passengers disembarked. As the boat backed away from the dock one of the passengers realized that he had left a bag on the boat and excitedly yelled to the crew. Without missing a beat, Shawn Raines brought the boat around and quickly docked it to the relief of the forgetful traveler. Within seconds the *Lady Express* was heading toward Chelan. By now most of the passengers had settled down in their seats and were anxious to get back to Chelan. Several sought out Nancy Clapp's advice about places to eat or routes out of town. She cheerfully fulfilled every request for information. Soon the *Lady Express* slid into the dock at 4:20 p.m. and the crew quickly tied the craft

Ladies of the Lake

Lady Express heading home

to her berth. Weary, but thankful passengers then filed off the boat buoyed by Nancy's final good wishes.

Besides her duties as a passenger boat the *Lady Express* also does its share of charters. Like the *Lady of the Lake II* the express boat hosts many classes of graduating high school seniors every spring. Student field trips up lake are also another of the *Lady Express's* many charters. One such trip was made by a group of first, second, and third graders from Chelan Elementary in May of 1998. The previous fall the students and their teachers (Vicki Anderson, Barb Marney, and Kathie Teeley) had produced and sold a local history calendar and used the profits to charter the *Lady Express* for a day trip to Stehekin. The Chelan students had been corresponding with Stehekin teacher, Ron Scutt, and his students and were anxious to meet them. The *Lady Express* and her crew made the excursion a trip of a lifetime for the young Chelan students.

New Lady, 1998

The newest addition to the Lake Chelan Boat Company fleet will be a swift, catamaran style vessel. The craft is scheduled to be finished and on the lake by late May of 1998, according to boat company owner Jack Raines. Shaw Boats of Hoquiam, Washington is building the catamaran that is expected to

The Boats, 1929-1998

An artist's conception drawing of the new Lady

cost around one million dollars. When completed the vessel will be fifty-one feet long with a sixteen foot beam. Twin 555 Caterpillar™ engines will propel the boat to a cruising speed of fifty miles per hour. At this speed the boat will be able to make the trip to Stehekin in seventy-five minutes. Keeping with tradition, the boat company is sponsoring a "name the boat" contest for their newest Lady. Jack Raines hinted that entries which include "Lady" in them would be highly favored.

    The Lake Chelan Boat Company plans to have the swift craft in operation by the first part of June. Starting June 15 the boat company will run the catamaran to the head of the lake twice a day. The boat will leave from Chelan at 7:45 a.m. and at 1:30 p.m. and make return trips from Stehekin at 10:30 a.m. and 4:15 p.m. Stops will be made at Field's Point in both directions, but there will not be any flag stop service. The boat company plans to charge between sixty-five and seventy dollars for a round-trip ticket. "Everyone's vacation time is getting shorter or more precious. It's the '90s. People want to get up there. It's going to add so many different options for people," the boat company marketing director, Chris Raines, told the *Wenatchee World*. As always, building faster boats has been an integral part of the history of commercial passenger vessels on Lake Chelan.

Ladies of the Lake

Kit Hines (left) and Bob Langenbach heading to Stehekin in a steam powered launch, 1996

Section Five
• • • • • • •

The Big Wave

"I didn't have time to decide if it was a mirage or the Lady of the Lake sea monster."
Chris Raines, Lady of the Lake II pilot, May 1997

As the seventy foot monster wave came crashing toward the *Lady of the Lake II* the captain had to make a quick decision. The preceding sentence reads like the opening of a cheesy novel, but in this case truth really was stranger than fiction. When all was said and done there would be more questions than answers. While many people on the boat saw what appeared to be a large wave from miles away, whatever it was never lasted long enough to be seen up close. Just what was this phenomenon that appeared on Lake Chelan near Twenty Five Mile Creek on the afternoon of May 5, 1997? Could the wave have been caused by the fabled monster of Lake Chelan? Did an earthquake or underwater landslide trigger the large wave? Was it an optical illusion? Or did compressed gases suddenly release from the lake's bottom to give rise to a huge bubble that looked like a massive wave? There are several early reports and occurrences on the lake which support all these theories. We will never know what happened that day, but the event will always be remembered in Lake Chelan lore as simply — the Big Wave.

Just what did the crew of the *Lady of the Lake II* and the boat's passengers see that day? Probably the best account of what happened was published in the Summer 1997 issue of the *Stehekin Choice*. A seventh grade Stehekin School student, Chris Karapostoles, interviewed Todd Schnelle who had served as the *Lady II's* first mate the day of the big wave. A portion of that interview follows:

Ladies of the Lake

Chris [Karapostoles]: What did you [Todd Schnelle] see? What time and what location?

Todd: It was Monday, May 5, 1997. I was on board the *Lady of the Lake II* with Chris Raines [the boat's head pilot]. We had 207 passengers on board. It was a nice afternoon, probably about 70 degrees, and there was about a 5 to 10 mile an hour wind. We were directly across from Safety Harbor, and I looked downlake, and I noticed something very odd as far down the lake as I could see. When there is a lot of wind downlake from you, you can see the water shake, and it's kind of fuzzy, and at first that's all I thought it was. Then I picked up the binoculars and looked, and, down near Twenty Five Mile Creek, what I saw through the binoculars looked to us to be a big wave that was cresting. It looked to be coming directly at us, and our best guess at the time was that it was anywhere from 50 to 75 feet tall. I looked at it and I asked Chris Raines, who was the head pilot of the day, to look through the binoculars, not telling him what I saw. He said, "Oh my gosh, I think that's a wave!!!" We both looked at it several times, and deduced that if this in fact was a wave we would not be able to ride it out. The way it was crashing over itself, it would have come right over the top of us; and a wave that big would be coming fast, so we had to do something right away.

Chris: About how far away from it were you when you first saw it?

Todd: When we first saw it, we're guessing that it was about 7 to 10 miles away. As you know, that area in the [straits] you can see from Twenty Five Mile Creek up to Point No Point, which is about seventeen miles, so we figured about ten miles or so. From the size of the wave, we decided that it would be coming towards us pretty quick. We had some of the other passengers look at it through binoculars, and we heard a couple other people say, "That looks like a big wave!" For the safety of the 207 passengers on board, rather than turn around and outrun it, we decided to unload the passengers on the beach at Safety Harbor. Chris Raines

The Big Wave

Lady of the Lake II heading up lake

decided to put the boat up on the beach and off-load all the passengers onto the beach off the bow. So we pulled into Safety Harbor, put the gangplank down, and walked through the cabin trying to keep the passengers calm and walking towards the bow. We got everybody off onto the beach. From there I took a pair of binoculars and ran up onto the point to see if I could see downlake. In my head I was thinking, "If this wave is not here by now, it more than likely is not going to materialize." As big as it was, it had to been moving fast. I got as far as I could around the point of Safety Harbor, but I still couldn't see downlake. So I went back to the boat and we decided to back the boat out of the harbor to take a look and see what was happening. We backed the *Lady II* out into the lake, and what we had seen earlier was completely gone. So we pulled back in, picked up the passengers, and headed downlake. At this point, we were mainly looking for anything that would tell us that there had been a wave. But there were no swells coming up the lake, the wind hadn't changed, and when we got down

> to the Twenty Five Mile Creek area, and we looked at the shoreline with the binoculars and there was no wet shoreline, no downed trees, no wet beaches to indicate that there had been a large wave.
>
> And that's about all there is to the story. We did have four or five passengers who said that they saw exactly what we saw. To date we have no explanation for what we saw. We called the sheriff who called the University of Washington to see if there was any seismic activity. In the area there was a three point earthquake at about the same time, in Concrete, Washington, but that's quite a ways away from Lake Chelan. We talked about the optical illusions that can be on the lake at times, but neither Chris nor I, with about nineteen to twenty years of experience between us, have ever seen any optical illusion as large as the one we saw. The wave crested and rolled across the lake from the north shore to the south shore and then rolled again. We actually saw a tube form that rolled twice from left to right as this wave was coming up lake. But as I said before, the wind was blowing downlake, and when we got back onto the lake, there were no swells, no sign of a wave whatsoever.

Schnelle went on to explain that the passengers included a group of 180 high school students who were returning from their stay at Holden Village. Schnelle said that when the announcement was made that a wave was coming toward the boat some of the students began to panic. But after making a quick trip through the cabin, Schnelle was able to calm most of the passengers.

In an interview with Jeanette Marantos of the *Wenatchee World*, Todd Schnelle said that as the wave "moved on us ... It was not consistently the same height all the way across. In the middle it humped up like a surf wave would in Hawaii when it starts to crest, rolling left to right and then starting again. It was white water coming down ... rolling toward us all the while. We were very concerned." Chris Raines told Marantos that he made the Lake Chelan Boat Company's first emergency docking and unloading of passengers at Safety Harbor because of a grayish hump he saw inside the water. "That damn hump ... If there hadn't been that gray hump. You could see it without binoculars, and some of the passengers said they could see it too. It was moving from one side to the other, and I just assumed it was the core of whatever was happening down there, like maybe a giant air bubble from an underground aquifer. But I

The Big Wave

didn't have time to decide if it was a mirage or the Lady of the Lake sea monster," Raines said.

Lake Chelan monster stories have circulated in the Chelan Valley and beyond ever since the first indigenous people roamed the region. At least one Native American legend holds that the early inhabitants purposely dammed the foot of the lake to kill a marauding monster. According to the myth the monster did not die, but survived to inhabit the depths of the lake. Chelan Indian elders said that their early ancestors were never at ease near or on the lake. If the following story proved to be true, early white settlers should have been wary of Lake Chelan as well.

In the fall of 1892 the *Wilbur Register* reported that three travelers had recently gone to the head of Lake Chelan and camped at a place called Devil's Slide. One morning as one of the men was cleansing his feet in the lake he suddenly screamed to his partners that some unseen marine monster was holding his leg. When his friends pulled the man ashore, to their surprise a monster emerged from the depths still clinging to the man's leg with its teeth. The men described the horrid looking creature as having the legs and body of an alligator and the head and restless eyes of a serpent. "Between its fore and hind legs, on either side were large, ribbed, leathery looking wings. The tail was scaled, but not barbed like that in the picture of a typical dragon. With the exception of the under part of the throat and the tips of the wings, feet and tail, the creature was a beautiful white and its skin soft as velvet," the paper reported. In an attempt to extradite their friend's leg from the beast the men built a large fire and pulled the serpent's neck into the inferno while being careful not to burn the stricken man. In time the scorching heat aroused the strange animal and it stretched out its wings in a bat-like fashion and suddenly flew into the air while still clenching the man's leg. After rising to a height of about 200 feet the flying monster plunged straight down toward the lake and with a tremendous splash dove headlong into the water burying itself and the victim out of sight. The *Register* ended by reporting that the "local natives" were greatly excited and believed that the sighting of the "great white dragon" was a premonition of the end of the world. The story made for great drama, but local residents greatly doubted the veracity of this obvious tall tale. But such reports would fuel the imaginations of Chelan Valley residents for years to come.

Another Lake Chelan monster story made the rounds in 1905 when the *Leader* reported the sighting of a huge sea serpent at the head of the lake. Sam Campbell, John Waddel, and J. W. Budd reportedly saw a seventy-five foot long snakelike creature in the water just off of the Stehekin landing. Ben Little told the *Leader* that he too had seen the creature some weeks earlier. Captain E. E. Shotwell also admitted that he and his engineer had seen the monster snake

Ladies of the Lake

twice while on mail runs to the head of the lake. Supposedly, Shotwell and the engineer were very reluctant to talk about the incidents. The *Leader* editorialized that the reports were most likely hoaxes, but admitted that maybe there was something to all the Lake Chelan monster speculation.

When the school bus accident occurred in 1945 there were rumors that bell-helmeted divers spotted a fish larger than any man. Indians believed this proved the existence of a monster. Countless other stories abound about odd creatures that have been spotted or bumped the undersides of boats, but no one ever seriously suggested that a sea serpent or the like caused the most recent monster wave.

Another explanation for the huge wave was the possibility that an earthquake or underwater rock slide caused it. Although the University of Washington reported that there was no earthquake activity in the vicinity of Lake Chelan that day, it is not the first time that local residents suspected that seismic forces might have generated a large wave. The first reported case happened on an otherwise dead calm day in September of 1899. It is not known what caused the wave, but one theory was that a huge underwater rock slide may have produced the phenomenon. The thinking at the time was that volcanic upheaval inland might have triggered such a rock slide. Judge I. A. Navarre, who was ten miles up Twenty Five Mile Creek when it happened, said that prospectors in the area declared that the creek went dry for three hours.

The mysterious wave sunk the steamer *Kitten,* just below Twenty Five Mile Creek. The Kitten was docked near E. F. Christie's place, located on the south shore about nineteen miles up lake, when a six to ten foot wave hit her. J. A. Graham watched as the action threw the craft onto the rocks and then saw the receding waves capsize and sink the boat. Succeeding waves of diminishing strength continued for over two hours. Thomas Gibson said that at Mountain Park, only four miles to the southeast, the waves were only one foot high. The crew of the steamer *Dexter*, which later helped raise the *Kitten*, reported that the wave had been very noticeable at Moore Point and at Stehekin.

Locals later claimed that several years prior to this wave surveyors had used a wire and weight to determine that the lake depth was over 1600 feet at its deepest. When the depth was measured again in the same area, many years after the 1899 wave, it measured close to the official depth of 1,486 feet. Some theorists said that this was evidence that a rock slide had filled in the bottom of the lake.

After the sinking of the *Kitten* local residents and vacationers reported other large waves on Lake Chelan during the years that followed. In June of 1903 a fishing party, which included County Assessor Osborn and G. A. Benson of Lakeside, sighted a large wave in the Prince Creek and Twin Harbor region

The Big Wave

of the lake. Six years later, also in June, fishermen camped at Twenty Five Mile Creek described their frightening experience to the *Leader*. Judge W. J. Long, his son-in-law, L. N. Bragg, and Long's friend, Harold Wetherland had set up their tent near the mouth of the creek. Early one morning a violent "quivering of his spring cot" shook the judge awake. When Long looked out the tent's opening he saw a six foot high wave moving across the "quiet surface" of the lake straight for his camp. Before he could react the wave slammed into the beach. The force of the wave threw his launch and other movable objects well above the water line. Long surmised that a "seismic shock" caused the phenomenon.

Although earthquakes made a compelling argument as to their role in generating large waves, lack of seismic activity near Lake Chelan that day in May of 1997 seemed to rule out a quake as the cause of the "Big Wave." Old-timers, who had worked for years on the lake, said that what appeared to be big waves were in reality optical illusions. Retired Lake Chelan boat pilot, Claude Southwick, told the *Mirror* and the *Wenatchee World* that he had seen the optical illusion effect of a big wave several times on Lake Chelan. When Southwick first saw it in the early 1950s he was on the *Lady of the Lake* with former pilot, Jack Ashby. At the time, they were in the straits heading towards Field's Point when they saw a "big huge undulating wave" coming up lake right at their boat. Also in the 1950s Southwick had been on the *Speedway* when a similar episode happened. He said, "I swear you could see a huge wall of water coming at you." Both times the size, of what appeared to be a the large wave, slowly diminished as the boats continued down lake. Southwick offered the *World* an explanation for the phenomenon called refraction, which is the bending of light rays. "When you get to Point No Point and look across toward Twenty Five Mile Creek, you've got a 16 to 17-mile straight-away there, but the earth curves about 6 inches for every mile so you're not actually seeing the shoreline. It's bent out of shape quite a bit. And if you get the right atmospheric pressure and a little humidity, you can see what looks like a humongous wave rolling toward you, and the closer it gets to you, it disappears." Southwick told the *Mirror* that refraction causes many weird visual anomalies. Once when Southwick was on a ship 150 miles out to sea from Tokyo, Japan he turned around and saw Mt. Fuji, "just as large as the Chelan Butte." He explained that this too was an example of bending light rays causing an optical illusion.

Even though Chris Raines knew the rationale supporting this optical illusion analysis, the memory of the crashing wave gnawed at him. Raines told Richard Uhlhorn of the *Lake Chelan Mirror*, "you know, I've been on this lake for 13 years... 11 as a captain. I've seen every optical illusion you can think of... I've been in white outs, black outs, had lightning hit the water in front of our

Ladies of the Lake

barge with a full load of fuel... I've been out in winds up to 100 mile per hour and this looked like it was curling. It could have been an air bubble." If it was a bubble how could one as large as the one Raines saw be generated? In theory melting snow recharging the water table could force air down deep into the ground water table which could cause a big bubble. Such a bubble could rise from the lake bed and expand at the surface into a radiating curling wave. When the bubble finally breaks through the surface water tension it disappears without disturbing the shoreline.

An air bubble was not only theoretically possible, but it may have happened before on Lake Chelan. At approximately 4:45 p.m. on Saturday July 21, 1906, residents at Deer Point and those down and across the lake near Twenty Five Mile Creek reported observing a strange sight. This is what the *Leader* reported under the headline — The Lake "Bubbles" Again:

> **The water appeared to rise up like the roof of a house off the point [Deer], and near the point it seemed to boil. A thin vapor floated across to the opposite shore. The water slid upon the shore in large waves on each side of the point and back again several times. The disturbance lasted for over half an hour. The lake was very still, before the occurrence except for a sight ripple.**
>
> **If any other parties observed the phenomenon, please report. As the residents of Rosedale [near Twenty Five Mile Creek] ... who saw it are not addicted to drinking anything stronger than lake water, there was no optical illusion in this case.**

The article did not explain anything about the lake bubbling on a previous occasion, but the headline clearly implied that it had happened before. There were not any further reports found about the incident in later issues of the *Leader*.

When the 1997 "big wave" appeared at least one other person, not on the *Lady of the Lake II*, reported seeing it. A man called Chelan County sheriff's deputies at about 5:00 p.m. to say he saw a "giant wave." The Sheriff's Office later told a reporter from the *Wenatchee World* that their deputies could not confirm that a big wave had occurred. Alvin Anderson, who manages the D & G Peterson orchard near Green's Landing, was working near the lakeshore about the time the *Lady II's* crew saw the wave. Anderson claims that he and three of his workers observed the lake level quickly raise over two feet and then recede back to normal. At the time Anderson and his crew were working in front of a lakeside home owned by Gail Boyd, who is a part-owner of the D & G Peterson orchard. Anderson, a lifelong Chelan Valley resident, said

The Big Wave

Looking down lake towards the Deer Point area

Ladies of the Lake

Alvin Anderson standing above the portion of the lake he said raised over two feet in a matter of seconds

there was no boat traffic at the time and that the lake was calm. He theorized that an underwater landslide may have caused a disturbance above Twenty Five Mile Creek and that the curvature of the lake down from Field's Point might be the reason the water rose noticeably on the north shore near Green's Landing. Longtime Twenty Five Mile Creek residents, Keith and Alice Marney, said that they were outside working in the yard of their lakefront home when the wave activity reportedly took place. Neither saw anything out of the ordinary that day other than a light breeze and a slight chop on the lake. "Even as deaf as I am, I am sure I would have heard it if a tidal wave hit our beach," Keith later joked.

Like all of the other strange phenomena reported to have occurred on Lake Chelan, what caused the latest "Big Wave" will probably never be known. There will always be theories and explanations by old-timers as to why the lake behaves the way she does. That is what makes the Lake Chelan experience unique. Just remember to keep a sharp eye out while on or near the lake, because the next giant wave or marauding sea monster could be heading your way.

Epilogue

This accounting of old boats, barges, big waves, and the like could make one squeamish about riding on today's passenger boats. You should not be. Even with all the fires, sinkings, and other mayhem that was a major part of the early era of boating on Lake Chelan — a simple fact remains. In the one hundred and nine years of Lake Chelan passenger boat operations not a single passenger's life has been lost. This is a truly remarkable accomplishment when you consider the tremendous number of people who have traveled on commercial boats since 1899 (in 1997 the Lake Chelan Boat Company had its largest round-trip count ever at 35,000 passengers).

The early boats framed much of the history of the Chelan Valley. They connected its people while creating a thriving community. Today the boats provide a unique experience and service for both residents and tourists. The boats, and the men and women who contribute to their valuable presence, will always be a vital part of Lake Chelan.

Glossary of Boating Terms

Aft	close to, or toward the stern or the back of a boat or ship.
Amidships	in or toward the middle of a boat or ship.
Beam	the extreme width of a boat.
Bow	the front end of a vessel.
Bulkhead	a wall-like construction inside a boat which provide watertight compartments or strengthen the structure.
Capstan	any of various windlasses, rotated in a horizontal plane by hand or machinery, for winding in ropes or cables.
Catamaran	a boat whose frame is set on two parallel hulls.
Draft	the depth to which a vessel is immersed when bearing a given load.
Engineer	the officer in charge of, or who operates the vessel's engines.
Fore	at or toward the front of a vessel.
Hull	the hollow lowermost portion of a boat, floating partially submerged and supporting the remainder of the boat.
Keel	a central fore-and-aft structural member in the bottom of a boat's hull extending from the stem to the stempost.
Launch	a heavy open or half-decked boat propelled by oars or by an engine.
Prow	the front part of a boat or ship.
Purser	an officer who is in charge of the accounts and documents of a boat and who keeps money and valuables for the passengers.

Ladies of the Lake

Rudder   a vertical blade at the stern of a vessel that can be turned to change the vessel's direction when in motion.

Schooner   any of the various types of sailing vessels having a foremast and mainmast.

Screw   boat propeller.

Stem   an upright structure at the bow of a vessel into which the side timbers or plates are joined.

Stern   the back or rear of a boat.

Sternwheeler   a boat propelled by a paddle wheel at the stern.

Wheel   a circular frame with an axle connecting to the rudder of a boat, for steering.

Bibliography

Manuscript Materials

Chelan Museum Notebooks. Chelan, Washington.

Greene, Bernice, Papers. Photostatic copies available in the Local History section of the Wenatchee Public Library and the North Central Washington Museum.

King, Albion L. *Memories of the Early Days in the Entiat Valley.* Typewritten manuscript, 1966.

Klement, Otto. *Early Skagit Recollections.* Typescript manuscript, Mount Baker National Forest, Seattle, Washington, 1935.

Larrabee, Myrtle. *The Use of Local Photographic Material in the Development of Social Studies Units for the Intermediate Grades.* Master's Thesis, Ellensburg, WA: Central Washington College of Education, 1950.

Mitchell, Bruce. *Camp Chelan, 1879-1880.* Typescript manuscript, Local History section of the Wenatchee Public Library.

Shoemaker, Allen, Papers. Photostatic copies in possession of the author.

Smith, John H. *Orondo: As I Knew It.* Typewritten manuscript, 1976.

Whaley, Myrtle, Papers. Originals in the possession of Al Boyd, Chelan, Washington.

Federal Documents

Luxenberg, Gretchen. *Historic Resource Study North Cascades National Park Service Complex Washington.* Cultural Resources Division. Pacific Northwest Region. National Park Service. Department of the Interior, 1986.

United States Army Commands. Camp Chelan and Camp Spokane, Washington Territory, Letters Sent, August, 1879 - December, 1880. National Archives, Record Group 98. Typewritten copies found in the John Brown Papers.

Articles

"Chelan County, Washington." *Wilhelm's Magazine The Coast.* Vol. VXII, No. 4, October, 1906.

Ladies of the Lake

Denny, E. I. "Chelan: A Wonderful Lake of the Cascade Range." *The Northwest Illustrated Monthly Magazine.* Vol. 14, No. 6, June, 1896.

Downing, Alfred. "A Trip to Lake Chelan." *West Shore.* Vol. 15, No. 173, September 28, 1889.

Hutson, Pat. "Snow-Mantled Stehekin: Where Solitude is in Season." *National Geographic.* Vol. 145, April, 1974.

"Lake Chelan a Summer Resort." *Wilhelm's Magazine The Coast.* Vol. VIII, No. 3, December, 1904.

McKinstry, Bruce L. and Klamm, Allis McKay. "A Frontier Childhood." *Lake Chelan History Notes,* Spring, 1975.

Park, Edwards. "Washington Wilderness, the North Cascades." *National Geographic.* Vol. 119, March, 1961.

Rodman, Samuel. "Exploration in the Upper Columbia Country." *Overland Monthly.* Vol. VII. 2nd Series, March, 1886.

Sperlin, O. B. "Exploration of the Upper Columbia." *Washington Historical Quarterly.* Vol. IV. No. 1, January, 1913.

"The Steamer 'Chelan.'" *Lake Chelan History Notes,* Spring, 1974.

Wakefield, Pierre. "Pictures of Places." *Wilhelm's Magazine The Coast.* Vol. VI, No. 3, October, 1901.

Books and Pamphlets

Adams, Nigel B. *The Holden Mine: Discovery to Production.* Wenatchee, WA: Washington State Historical Society, 1981.

Affleck, Edward Lloyd. *Affleck's List of Sternwheelers and Other Larger Steamboats Working on the Columbia River Waterways North of the 47th Parallel of Latitude 1865-1965.* Vancouver, British Columbia: Alexander Nicolls Press, 1993.

Anderson, Eva. *Rails Across the Cascades.* Wenatchee, WA: World Publishing Company.

Beardslee, Daniel E. *An Investigation of the Historic Ordinary High Water Elevation of Lake Chelan.* Brewster, WA: Erlandsen and Associates, 1992.

Bibliography

Byrd, Robert. *Lake Chelan in the 1890's*. Wenatchee, WA: Bryd-Song Publishing, 1992.

Carpenter, Marcelle. *Alfred LaChapelle: From Pointe to Point*. Bonney Lake, WA: Lake Jane Press, 1996.

Chelan High School Annual, 1913. Chelan, WA: Lake Chelan School District, 1913.

Dow, Edson. *Passes to the North*. Wenatchee, Washington, 1963.

Ekman, Leonard. *Scenic Geology of the Pacific Northwest*. Portland, OR: Binfords & Mort, 1962.

Ficken, Robert E. and LeWarne. *Washington: A Centennial History*. Seattle: University of Washington Press, 1988.

Hackenmiller, Tom. *Wapato Heritage: The History of the Chelan and Entiat Indians*. Manson, WA: Point Publishing, 1995.

Holden Mine: Largest Copper Producer in the Northwest. Holden, WA: F. H. Brogan.

Hull, Lindley, ed. *A History of Central Washington*. Spokane: Shaw and Borden Company, 1929.

McConnell, Grant. *Stehekin, A Valley in Time*. Seattle: The Mountaineers, 1988.

McGill, Marthalene Filley, ed. *Bits and Pieces of Pioneer Life: Around Lake Chelan, Washington*. Youngtown, AZ: Sun City - Youngtown Printers, 1974.

Mills, Randall V. *Sternwheelers Up Columbia*. Palo Alto, CA: Pacific Books, 1947.

Mitchell, Bruce. *By River, Trail and Rail*. Wenatchee, WA: The Wenatchee Daily World, 1968.

Newell, Gordon R. *Ships of the Inland Sea*. Portland, OR: Binfords & Mort, 1951.

Newell, Gordon R. and Williamson, Joe. *Pacific Steamboats*. New York: Bonanza Books, 1958.

Paull, Gary. *Reflections of Lake Chelan*. Seattle: Pacific Northwest National Parks & Forests Association.

Ramsey, Guy Reed. *Postmarked Washington: Chelan, Douglas and Kittitas Counties*. Wenatchee, WA: The Wenatchee World, 1973.

Robertson, Gay. *Stehekin Remembered*. Seattle: Pacific Northwest National Parks & Forests Association, 1987.

Roe, JoAnn. *Stevens Pass*. Seattle: The Mountaineers, 1995.

Roe, JoAnn. *The North Cascadians*. Seattle: Madrona Publishers, 1980.

Ross, Alexander. *Adventures of the First Settlers on the Oregon or Columbia River*. London, Smith, Elder and Company, 1849.

Stanford, Wayne. *Glimpses of Manson History*. Wenatchee, WA: Frontier Publishing, 1993.

Steele, Richard F. *An Illustrated History of the Big Bend*. Spokane, Western Historical Publishing Company, 1904.

Steele, Richard F. *History of North Washington*. Spokane: Western Historical Publishing Company, 1904.

Stone, Carol M. *Stehekin: Glimpses of the Past*. Friday Harbor, WA: Long House Printcrafters and Publishers, 1983.

Taxelius, Tom. *St. Andrews Episcopal Church: The Early Years*. Chelan, WA: St. Andrew's Episcopal Church, 1995.

The Lady of the Lake (promotional material). Chelan, WA: Lake Chelan Boat Company, 1996.

Wapato Point History. Manson, WA: Wapato Point Resort promotional material, n.d.

Wilkes, Charles, U.S.N. *Narrative of the United States Exploring Expedition During the years 1838, 1839, 1840, 1841, 1842*. Vol. 4. Philadelphia, 1845.

Newspapers

Chelan Falls Leader, Chelan Falls, Washington.

Chelan Leader, Chelan, Washington.

Chelan Valley Mirror, Chelan, Washington.

Lakeside Light, Lakeside, Washington.

Orondo News, Orondo, Washington.

Bibliography

Stehekin Choice, Stehekin, Washington.

Wenatchee Daily World, Wenatchee, Washington.

Wenatchee Republic, Wenatchee, Washington.

Wenatchee World, Wenatchee, Washington.

Yakima Herald, Yakima, Washington.

Interviews and Lectures

Greene, Bernice, Interviews. Photostatic copies available in the Local History section at the Wenatchee Public Library.
    James Lindston, Chelan, Washington, Spring, 1976.

Hackenmiller, Tom, Interviews.
    Alice Adams, Chelan, Washington, January 9, 1998.
    Alvin Anderson, Manson, Washington, February 16 and 17, 1998.
    Bill and Mary Bigelow, Chelan, Washington, December 14, 1997.
    Steve Byquist, Chelan, Washington, December 15, 1997.
    Nancy Clapp, Chelan, Washington, February 11, 1998.
    Jim Courtney, Stehekin, Washington, February 11, 1998.
    Cindy (Raines) Engstrom, Chelan, Washington, February 1 and March 20, 1998.
    Evan and Myrt Griffith, Chelan, Washington, January 18, 1998.
    Betty Lust, Chelan, Washington, October 13, 1997.
    Barb and Mark Marney, Chelan, Washington, December 27, 1997.
    Keith Marney, Twenty Five Mile Creek, Washington, February 5, 1998.
    Patty (Pennell) Risley, Chelan, Washington, February 4 and March 12, 1998.
    Lydia Rivers, Wenatchee, Washington, October 27, 1997.
    Sandra Scribner, Chelan, Washington, December 16, 1997.
    Claude R. Southwick, Chelan, Washington, February 17, 1998.
    Ken Wilsey, Chelan, Washington, February 11, 1998.

Karapostoles, Chris, Interview, *Stehekin Choice*.
    Todd Schnelle, Stehekin, Washington, Summer 1997.

Layman, William. *"Captain Alexander Griggs and His Steamboats."* Lecture, North Central Washington Museum, Wenatchee, Washington, October 27, 1997.

Shoemaker, Allen, Interview. Allen Shoemaker Papers.
    Art Mathers, Chelan, Washington, n.d.

Boat Index

A

Abe Perkins 69
Allen Stone (1946) 131-133

B

Bailey Gatzert 22
Belle of Chelan (1889) 18, 21-30
Belle of Chelan (1905) 18, 75-80
Blackfoot Barge 96-99

C

Camano 70
Cascade Flyer (1921) 18, 107-111
Charlotte Mary 103
Chechahko (1903) 18, 72-75
City of Ellensburgh 22, 26, 44-45
City of Omaha (1890) 18, 30-33
Clipper (1891) 18, 33-35
Columbia 61
Columbia Queen 36
Comanche (1915) 18, 95-101
Comet (1910) 18, 85-87
Copper Queen 94
Corona 85

D

Discoverer 140
Dragon 109
Dragon / Dexter (1893) 18, 38-43

E

E. B. Schley (1937) 120-125
Enigma 69

F

Flyer (1902) 18, 69-72

G

Greyhound 22
Imp 62, 70

K

Kitten 158

L

Lady Express (1990) 18, 141-150
Lady of the Lake (1900) 18, 55
Lady of the Lake (1945) 18, 125-131
Lady of the Lake II (1976) 18, 134-141
Lady, New (1998) 18, 150-151
Lena (1913) 88
Liberty (1918) 18, 105-106

M

Maid of Mountain Park 33
Manson to First Creek Ferry - the Chief (1914) 88-90
Mascot 69
May Bell / Princess (1914) 18, 90-91
Mayflower 33
Miss Coulee 125-126
Mohawk (1916) 18, 101-104
Moore 94
Mount Royal 43
Mountain Queen 22
Mountaineer 39
Myrju 110, 116

173

Ladies of the Lake

N

North Star 73

O

Ona 85

P

Panama 93-94
Prosperity 39

Q

Queen of Chelan (1892) 18, 35-38

R

Radio 131
Rena 86-87
Rustler 32
Ruth 55

S

Scout 109
Selkirk 58
Speedway (1929) 18, 113-120
Spokane (1915) 18, 92-94
Stehekin (1894) 18, 43-51
Swan (1897) 18, 51-54

T

Tenino 105, 109, 114
Tourist (1906) 18, 80-84
Tramp 87
Tuttle Barge (1922) 111-112

V

Vagabond 94
Vashon 56
Victory (1919) 18, 106-107

W

Wanda (early 1920s) 104
Whippet 109

About the Author

Tom Hackenmiller and his wife, Kathie Teeley, have lived on Wapato Point since 1988. The beauty and rich history of the Chelan Valley has inspired Tom to try and preserve some of its many interesting stories. Beside *Ladies of the Lake*, the author has written another book about the Valley entitled *Wapato Heritage: The History of the Chelan and Entiat Indians*. Tom has a Masters Degree in History from Central Washington University in Ellensburg. His masters project dealt with the early history of the town of Ellensburg and Kittitas County. He has taught History at the college, secondary, and elementary levels.